THE

REAL

GLOW UP

A STEP-BY-STEP GUIDE FOR HOW YOU
CAN GLOW FROM THE INSIDE OUT

CHELSEY ARMFIELD

CONTENTS

The Real Glow Up Is When . . .

Preface

For the majority of my life, I felt lost. I could never understand why; things simply felt off. I didn't truly know how to love myself, trust myself, or take care of myself. I thought *messy* and *big* feelings were inconvenient and a sure indicator of my inherent weakness, so naturally I shoved them all the way down. Tending to someone else's needs instead of my own always felt more comfortable to me. Being a die-hard people pleaser, the mere thought of setting boundaries in my relationships sounded terrifying. While striving for goals, I pushed myself beyond my personal limits every single time, always coming from a place of shame and a never-good-enough mindset, which often left me riddled with anxiety. From the outside looking in, I was succeeding in life. However, my inner and outer world was not in alignment. I never felt like I was good enough, smart enough, or loveable enough, no matter what I was able to accomplish. Overtime, I grew accustomed to these negative feelings. These were the necessary sacrifices for a successful life, or so I believed.

Because of my neglected inner life, I attracted numerous dysfunctional friendships that often confirmed these same beliefs I held regarding my self-worth. They echoed the painful sentiments I felt deep down. These harmful friendship dynamics further blinded me to the fact that a healthier lifestyle existed. I mistook the harmful criticism for tough love. I endured insidious silent treatments and considered it to be proper reprimand. I kept quiet when I was purposely left out of plans, rationalizing these hurtful acts as accidental or warranted. And strangely enough, walking on eggshells and denying my experiences only prompted me to fight harder to maintain these damaging friendships. My misguided attempts at trying to be more accepted or valued always failed, as if "being more lovable" was the remedy.

My heart breaks for the younger version of myself—how she treated herself and allowed others to treat her. I'm pleased to share that this is no longer my truth. It took painful realizations, hardships, countless therapy sessions, radical self-compassion, and distancing myself from harmful friendships to finally understand my worth was hidden there all along. I recognize I'm not alone in this struggle. I know there are people who can relate to my story and who can benefit from these insights. I've worked hard to heal my inner world and to glean the necessary information in order to cultivate self-love and, ultimately, live a life I am proud of. I feel passionate about sharing this information with others on the off chance it helps another person do the same. I want you to feel encouraged to heal your trauma, to lay down a solid foundation built on self-compassion, to step into your truth, and to live your best life.

In a world where toxic positivity and hustle culture is pushed onto the masses (with the award going to the busiest), and where it's highly encouraged to do more while feeling less, I feel it is imperative to share this wisdom with you. True success does not come from running yourself into the ground, minimizing your needs, and hiding from your honest feelings. Self-neglect is not sustainable for anyone. Not to mention, a rushed and emotionally numb lifestyle serves as a catalyst and breeding ground for the crippling anxiety so many of us have been experiencing.

You may have heard the popular term "glow up," and if you aren't familiar with it, this phrase references a noticeable change in one's appearance (picture someone having a drastic makeover). Society tends to celebrate physical beauty without hesitation. Therefore, it is not hard to understand why we instinctively make outward appearance such a high priority in our lives. However, to look "good" does not necessarily equate to *feeling good*. There's so much more that goes into our well-being than how we physically appear to others. I want to share with you in this book what I believe to be *the real* "glow up."

We all have hopes and dreams, and those who create space for taking care of themselves while working toward their goals have a much stronger foundation to build upon. Those who are gracious and compassionate with themselves also receive another perk: the stamina to outlast others. This school of thought is the very nature of this book. Sharing the foundational steps of what I know to be *the real glow up* will allow you the chance to tap into your full potential and live a life that feels authentic to who you are at your core. Believe it or not, you *can* achieve your goals from a place of self-love and balance. You *can* toss out the stale, shame-based notion of "no pain no gain." This does not mean you won't ever experience discomfort on your journey. In fact, discomfort is an unavoidable part of growth and life in general. However, I assure you there is purpose and wisdom in this version of discomfort. In hindsight, you'll discover that your hardest moments were instrumental in leading you to your hard-earned peace, confidence, and overall fulfillment.

In a time when it seems the world operates on information overload, I want this to be a safe space where you can reflect on the decisions you've made and continue to make for your life. After all, you only have one life. Make your years and moments count. Design a life you are truly proud of and fully enjoy. Note the key word is *design*, because an intentional life takes thoughtful reflection, dedication, and patience. I will guide you through the design process in this book.

Your pain, trauma, fear, uncertainty, "crazy dreams," and messy and confusing feelings are all welcome here. You, as you are today, in whatever place in life you may be, are welcome here. I believe you deserve to feel your very best, to heal from whatever holds you back, and to live a life that feels authentic to you. I believe you have everything within you to make the lasting changes necessary to transform your life from the inside. I believe in you and hope that by the end of this book, you come to believe in yourself and feel empowered to work on the areas of your life that could use a little "rewrite." Because the truth is, your story isn't finished yet; your story is simply beginning a new chapter, and it's filled with radical self-love and an inspiring fresh start.

Introduction

In this book, I'm going to share how you can build a solid foundation filled with self-love and self-care—a foundation you can then build your dream life upon. But before we get to that, I think it's important to have an idea of what your ideal life looks like. Can you close your eyes and envision where you are, what you are doing, and who you have around you? Can you play out a day in your mind as if it's the best feel-good movie you've ever watched? For some, they can absolutely do this without hesitation. For others, they may have a bit of an idea of what their dream life would look like, but they haven't taken the time to piece it together or truly believe in their vision. You may feel lost, overwhelmed with an unending to-do list, and swept up in the currents of life, unable to find the paddle. Wherever you are, it's not too late to visualize your ideal life. It's okay if this is new to you. I've found that through experience, getting clear on our goals, and saving a bit of mental space for some playful, stress-free daydreaming, we are essentially opening the door to these opportunities. Creating a beautiful and inspiring vision gives us something to work toward—a purpose.

When you get clear on what you want, you subconsciously start to align your day-to-day decisions with those goals. Having clarity on how you envision your future also makes it clear what you don't want. At first, your life won't feel like it is changing substantially. Then one day, you actually find yourself working in a career you love that brings you fulfillment. You realize you are living in a cozy home, decorated just how you like it, surrounded by loving and supportive relationships. You are on a plane, traveling to your dream destination. You are actively making plans to marry and start a family. You get to choose your dream life. There are no rules here. For all I know, your ideal home is a quaint little cottage in a small town, and your desired career is crocheting blankets to sell at your local farmer's market. I feel it's important to clarify this is not a one-size-fits-all approach where I preach the commercialized American dream of owning fancy cars, a huge house, a boat, designer purses—you get it. Not everyone's dream life fits this narrative, and if it does, that's completely fine too. (I certainly dream about having a vacation home on a beach somewhere.) Chances are, if you picked up this book, you want a healthy balance of both internal and external success. The point being, these dreams now have the space to grow. Throughout this book, my goal is to assist you in creating a life that feels authentic to you. You deserve all the happiness, all the healing, all the growth, all the support, and all the success. My goal is to help you set a solid foundation so that these dreams have the space to transpire and flourish.

I think it's important to highlight that we all come from different backgrounds with varying advantages, disadvantages, injustices, and privileges. I do not want to minimize or dismiss anyone's struggles. I'm not here to suggest that if everyone applies the same amount of effort, they will have equal opportunity when striving for their goals. (I wish that were true, and I hope with my whole heart that one day we live in a world where there is equal opportunity for all.) However, no matter where you stand, I want you to know that you deserve to live a life you are proud to call your own.

I believe wholeheartedly that we each have a purpose to fulfill on Earth. We were brought here for a reason; therefore our life has meaning. Whether that be through parenthood, career, creative pursuits, advocacy, charitable work, or just being a genuinely kind person who makes others around them feel loved. You deserve to align with your highest self and live out the life that best suits your calling.

Throughout this book, as we lay the groundwork for your healthy foundation, there will be mini exercises at the end of each chapter. Most of the time you'll be asked to reflect on a specific area of your life. The exercises will serve as a guide on how you can take practical action and apply the suggestions in each chapter to your current situation. (If you don't own a journal, I would suggest purchasing one. Doing so will create a space where you can write out your responses to the prompts and reflect back on these teachable moments. Alternatively, you can use the Notes app on your phone and turn on the privacy feature if you don't want anyone coming across your thoughts.)

My promise to you is that by reading these chapters, by being honest with yourself, and by believing in your potential and the bigger picture, you can begin to step further into your truth and live the life you've always deserved. There is so much more to life than just getting by, and I want you to experience the fullness of what life has to offer you. An authentic life should be unapologetic and uncaged, free from fear, judgment, uncertainty, comparison, complacency, and compromising your dreams for convenience or out of habit. I hope this book stirs you up on the inside and gives you a beautiful, hopeful picture of what your life could be and will be. Begin to realize how worthy you are in this moment. Self-acceptance begins when you can love each phase you are in.

Let's dust off the areas that may need a little TLC because they've been overlooked or forgotten. It's time to set the very foundation that will support you in living your best life. You can't build a big, beautiful house on a weak foundation, no matter how beautiful the home. When you prioritize your mental health and self-care, you are finally making room for fresh, new opportunities to transpire. So let's start building, shall we?

1

The Real Glow Up Is When . . .

You Monitor How Full Your Cup Is

You may have heard the saying, "You cannot pour from an empty cup." This powerful phrase refers to the idea that in order to adequately show up for others, you must have the capacity to give. In other words, if you aren't properly taking care of yourself and your own needs (mentally, emotionally, physically, and spiritually), you are actually preventing yourself from the opportunity to better serve others. For example, you may visualize a cup so full of self-love, adequate rest, and a general sense of well-being that the "goodness" spills over onto the relationships that surround you. Sometimes society preaches the notion that you need to put others first, no matter what, at any cost. However, the "fill your cup" concept highlights the need to put yourself first, which then allows you to have the capacity to better show up for the people in your life. This insight is crucial yet overlooked by many (or sometimes learned and then not applied).

Filling up your cup can mean various things, such as resting more when you know it's needed, fueling your body with more fruits and vegetables to feel healthier, prioritizing exercise by walking outside and moving more, or choosing to soak in some inspirational content when your passion feels like it's fading. It might require watching a comedy and laughing because you know you have been taking life a little too seriously. It might mean journaling to get your unresolved thoughts out. Filling your cup can mean spending time alone because you've been around people all week, leaving you feeling drained. Maybe it's choosing to create something because you find joy in the simple act of tapping into your creative side. The possibilities are endless and are specific to whatever makes you feel the most whole and happy.

When you meet your own needs first, you are then able to give out of love and not obligation. You get to show up for people fully, anchored in your power. In my opinion, this is a beautiful form of being selfless. Help yourself first so that you can then share this compassionate, supportive, and loving energy with others. From this healthy mindset, you can then give others your very best self—a grade-A level of support. On an airplane, we are instructed to put on our oxygen masks first in case of an emergency, then we can help others second (even if it's our own child). *Boundaries* may seem like a buzzword these days, but maintaining them is an important self-protective life skill to understand and practice. Without setting healthy boundaries, you are subjecting yourself to unnecessary stress and anguish.

The reason I bring up self-care first is that many of us carry guilt when it comes to taking care of ourselves. It's important to understand the significance of self-care so you can read the following chapters with an open heart. You may have been taught to give all you have to others, no matter what. You may have people in your life who hint that you should feel guilty for not being there every moment they need you. You may be so used to putting others first that you've lost your sense of self, or perhaps you never developed a strong sense of self to begin with.

Trust me when I say you need to put down the guilt and prioritize your own self-care before addressing the needs of others. Not to mention, sometimes the reason people need you is because they aren't prioritizing their own self-care. This leads to you becoming a crutch for others, which only contributes to and perpetuates their problem. You are actually helping others when you set healthy boundaries and resist the urge to enable their harmful habits; you're simply letting this become someone else's problem from now on if they refuse to take accountability and make healthy life changes. (If you have a young child or infant, or you are a caretaker for someone, their constant need for you is valid. In this case, I'd urge you to be willing to find support, ask for help, and be sure to find small, realistic ways in which you can still show up for yourself in this phase of life to restore the balance.)

In some instances, people may ask for something, genuinely not knowing if you're in a good place to help them or not. A reasonable, unselfish person would rather you politely decline if you were overwhelmed or didn't have the capacity to help. It actually isn't fair to others if you say yes, despite you feeling worn down, because then you can't help but feel resentment for the situation. This results in a lose-lose situation. Only you can know your limits. Only you can gauge your gut reactions and know when, for example, that elaborate birthday party weekend is a good fit for you. Maybe a weekend partying would be a financial burden, or it might take away valuable time you need to rest and recharge. You are driving this train. You are in control, so you need to be honest and kind to yourself. "Your people" will understand and respect your needs, and if they don't, that is their issue, not yours. You may even start to reevaluate if they are truly your people once you gauge their reactions to your healthy boundary setting. (I'll speak more on that in a later chapter.)

On the flip side, if you invite others to attend something or ask for help in a specific area, please understand that it is their right to say no. People can explain as much or as little as they feel comfortable with, and sometimes you won't know the reasons behind why they decline. But please don't take their no personally. Respect their boundaries, and keep in mind that you don't know what they are going through or what their current needs are. I've learned this is hardly ever a reflection of how they see you or view your relationship; it's generally a personal matter that has absolutely nothing to do with you. Release the need to have answers for everything, and extend others grace and understanding. If you have continuous issues with this person and you think they might be purposefully keeping a distance or their saying no could be meant in a malicious or hurtful way, then by all means reevaluate the relationship. But you'll be able to intuit the difference as you inherit clearer boundaries yourself.

It Comes Down to Balance

Living a balanced life allows you the capacity to be there for yourself and others. It's the difference between living in desperation, anxiety, and lack versus living joyfully, excited, and empowered. You can't give more than you have—period. That's when the balance is thrown off. It may feel like a delicate balance at first, but it's worth it to pay attention and carefully take each scenario on a case-by-case basis, releasing all shame.

The simple act of taking a step back and observing will get easier over time. With some practice, it will begin to feel automatic. Mentally and emotionally healthy people will respect your boundaries without hesitation. You may notice that turning something or someone down has a trigger effect on some people. All you can do is send love their way by graciously thanking them for thinking of you, declining their offer (without feeling the need to overexplain your reason why), and simply let them work through the rest.

For those on the receiving end, boundaries can feel like abandonment to people with unhealthy attachment issues (you might even relate). It can feel scary and heavy for them to experience any perceived rejection. This typically goes back to their past experiences and perhaps traumas. Walking this fine line requires two things of you: being there for them while also letting them work through those feelings on their own. You cannot fix deep wounds in others, and you mustn't spend your life tiptoeing around their emotions and abandoning your truth for their sake. (Spoiler alert: no one wins when you do this anyway.)

Healthy Boundaries Versus Flaking

Being mindful of what events you choose to attend isn't to promote flakiness. If you commit to something, then try your best to honor that commitment. If you know that going is not what's best for you because of unexpected life circumstances that steer you in a different direction (which can certainly happen), please be thoughtful as to how this affects the other person and how you communicate declining the invite. For example, if I commit to a birthday party, then when the day arrives and I'm feeling really fatigued, or if I'm experiencing a challenging mental health day, I may bring a thoughtful gift and make a brief appearance versus spending hours at the party. Or, if attending is simply out of the question, I will send the host a kind message as far ahead of time as possible to let them know I would love to attend but unfortunately something came up. (A little bit of tact and polite communication here goes a long way.)

The next time you get an invite, buy yourself some time and say, "Thank you for thinking of me. I'll check my schedule and get back to you." Then think about whether you really want to attend, reminding yourself that there is no obligation to overextend yourself if your plate is full. Personally, I would prefer someone being honest with me from the beginning rather than cancelling two hours prior because they felt the need to people please in the moment and RSVP a yes without actually thinking it through. If you don't know how to politely decline, you can always say, "I'm sorry I won't be able to make it, but thank you so much for the invite." It's really that simple, though it sometimes feels like we need to offer a concrete reason as to why we can't make it to something. People pleasing comes from a well-intentioned place, but we need to advocate for ourselves without our needs becoming something to feel shameful about. This fill-your-cup notion all comes back to what I mentioned previously . . .

Laying Your Foundation

With a strong foundation, you are empowered enough to handle what life throws your way with more ease. Because let's face it, life is messy at times, and handling these surprises with a calm demeanor is the ultimate goal so that we can dedicate our valuable energy toward the things we are passionate about. You can't have a strong foundation without consistent self-care. And you cannot engage in self-care without proper boundaries in place. Please give yourself permission to advocate for your own needs. You know yourself and your own limits best, and taking care of yourself is nothing to feel ashamed about.

Be Careful of the FOMO Trap

With social media and constant access to what many people are doing at any given moment, our culture has created the term FOMO (fear of missing out). This fear is predicated on the idea that you could always be doing more, which is a slippery slope for your mental and emotional well-being. We are blessed with so many opportunities to connect with others, grab dinner or coffee, network, attend events, and experience new and exciting things. But this all comes back to what state your cup is in. For example, don't force yourself to attend an event (or several) because you think that's what you are *supposed* to do. Get intentional about why you want to attend and weigh the pros and cons to see if it makes sense for you at that given moment. Life isn't a race or competition for who can do and achieve the most; it's about what's best for you in your current season of life. If you catch yourself getting distracted over what everyone else is doing and how often they are doing it, I encourage you to take a step back, take a deep breath, and remind yourself that your journey isn't going to look like everyone else's all the time (it's not supposed to). Your journey is tailored to your specific needs and goals at that given moment. Go at your own pace.

Mini Exercise

In the upcoming weeks, pay attention to what opportunities come up for you. Before committing to them, take a few minutes (or as long as you need) to pause, breathe, reflect, and evaluate if the opportunity makes sense for you right now. Maybe you can't commit quite yet and need some time to see how you feel about it later. Maybe it feels right but you know the days leading up to it are jam-packed. In this scenario, you will thank yourself later for anticipating your needs in advance by politely declining. Maybe you know it feels right and it is in line with your goals, yet the only thing holding you back is some social anxiety and fear of leaving your comfort zone. In that case, I encourage you to challenge yourself to walk through the discomfort and face your fears.

It's a fine balance, but with practice, this will all become second nature. You will feel empowered when you work with the flow of your life rather than swimming against it. Only you can advocate for this peaceful balance; no one can do it for you.

2

The Real Glow Up Is When . . .

You Begin to Notice Your Conditioning

Whether you realize it or not, the majority of our decisions and habits are deeply ingrained in us, beginning in childhood and continuing throughout adulthood, based on what we've been taught or exposed to—within family and friendship dynamics and through different cultures and societal norms. Let's take self-sabotage as an example of conditioning. I have always had the habit of getting really close to a goal of mine, or getting things started, and then for some reason pausing and stalling on ever completing that goal. There is no valid reasoning behind why I would cease to take the necessary actions to complete the task. This pattern drove me crazy because I could see how I was stopping myself from carrying out my goals, but I wasn't sure why I kept repeating the self-sabotage cycle. It was increasingly frustrating, and these situations created an abundance of shame. I began to think something was wrong with me, which only fed my negative thoughts and diminished my confidence even more.

I then began diving into the work of uncovering my limiting beliefs—the subconscious beliefs and ideas I had carried with me throughout my whole life. Deep down, I truly did not believe I deserved success or that I was worthy enough to achieve my goals. I was just as capable as anyone else, but my limited thinking (on a subconscious level) prevented me from moving forward. This is why it's helpful to process what beliefs sit right beneath the surface, ready to thwart our best-laid plans and intentions.

Some stories that frequently played in my head were:

- *Who do you think you are trying to accomplish this goal?*

- *You aren't good enough to be as successful as _____.*

- *There isn't enough room for you to succeed. It's an oversaturated work field.*

- *You don't deserve that level of success.*

- *You aren't good enough at _____.*

- *People will judge you, so don't do it.*

- *You don't know enough, so you'll likely embarrass yourself.*

Uncovering and rewriting these subconscious stories of mine have been life-changing. The first step is to slowly but surely silence your inner critic. Then, take the pen out of the critic's hand and rewrite the inner dialogue yourself, even if it feels counterintuitive to your belief system (because it is).

- *I am worthy of success.*

- *I deserve happiness.*

- *I am capable of helping others with my work.*

- *I am capable of accomplishing my dreams.*

- *I am allowed to shine.*

- *I don't have to play it safe.*

- *I will be okay if some people judge me.*

- *I don't need everyone else's approval.*

- *It's okay to be a beginner; everyone starts somewhere.*

- *I am brave for trying something new.*

When I started to make this change, it was like an invisible weight had been slowly lifted off my shoulders. The limiting beliefs I had known as truths were just my unrealized *conditioning*. I'm going to be honest with you: the healing process of rewriting faulty programming isn't an overnight one, especially if your inner critic is a real bully. Some of us have a fairly kind inner dialogue, but many of us have learned to be hard on ourselves as a means to keep up with this busy, overachieving, and constantly-striving-for-more mentality. It can be so automatic that you don't even realize you're doing it. These self-doubts may even be so ingrained in you that they feel factual, like simple logic, as if there is no way around these (albeit false) truths.

It's no wonder we are so hard on ourselves. Society generally encourages us to do more, be more, have more, and sacrifice it all. The "always doing more" mentality is a lie. You do not need to always be striving for more in order to be successful. The goal here is to shift your perspective a bit so you can recognize these destructive and limiting thoughts when they arise. Realize you are amazing whether you are performing and achieving or whether you are blowing off some steam by watching a reality TV show and checking out for a bit. Your worth is not something you need to earn; it is inherent and never leaves you. You've always been good enough, but now it's time to disassemble these negative and harsh thoughts in order to finally believe this truth.

Practicing Discernment

While rewriting your harmful conditioning, it's important to practice discernment in your day-to-day life. You may come across some things—online, on TV, or in your conversations with people—that are counterproductive to the new narrative you are choosing. This is why it's important to possess a certain level of discernment with what you are consuming. Otherwise, it's easy to fall into a trap of self-doubt and shame. For example, if you are starting to listen to your body and letting yourself rest more, and then you come across someone online who seems to be a high achiever who doesn't allow themselves the same level of self-care, you may experience thoughts like, *What am I doing on the couch right now? I feel so lazy and unproductive.* That's when you should remind yourself that you deserve rest. That working yourself too hard is not a marker of real success. You can be a high-achiever who practices self-care and operates from a healthy, balanced state. On the flip side, maybe lying on the couch watching TV doesn't feel helpful or restful to you, so instead ask yourself, "What could I be doing right now that would help me rest in a healthy, connected, and present way?" (Some examples are going for a walk, reading a chapter of a book, taking a hot bath, journaling, or calling a friend.) Again, the goal is to practice discernment because only you know what is best for you, and you need to stand firm in that regardless of what the outside world promotes. Please do not allow anyone, or any quote, or any other school of thought to open the door of shame into your life.

There are many harmful narratives that have been preached by society for a long time, and just because it's familiar doesn't make it true for you. That is for you to decide, not for you to absorb from other people who've not yet found balance or self-love in their own lives and, therefore, project their agenda onto you. Life is not one-size-fits-all, so you need to be careful not to compare your life to everyone else's.

Summary

Challenging and rewriting your subconscious beliefs is a learned practice and, as I mentioned, takes a bit of time to successfully pull off. This requires you to pay attention to your thoughts and to view them objectively, not as facts. When you examine your thoughts, slowly start to disassemble the harmful or limiting ones. Treat yourself like you would a best friend. What would you say to a best friend who is being too hard on themself or who is doubting their capabilities? Chances are, you would applaud them and would remind them they are a badass who is handling hard things while doing a fantastic job. You'd also remind them they deserve to take time for themself along the way.

You deserve those pep talks too—but from yourself. Take the time to replace your previous limiting beliefs with the new and beautiful truths that have always been there, but you weren't able to see before. As mentioned, this is a practice and takes time. Start wherever you are and, in time, you will heed beautiful results.

Mini Exercise

Take a moment to think about a lofty dream you may have. Now observe the fears that come into play when you think of this goal.

Notice if you have an inner critic who is running the show and discouraging you from even dreaming about it. Write down these limiting beliefs or fears. Some of mine used to be: "People will make fun of me." "I'm not qualified to do that." "I don't deserve to shine like that." "I'm not good enough." "What if I fail?"

Next, for every limiting belief, write down a response as if you were responding to your best friend, whom you believe in very much. Dissemble each thought and replace it with a kind truth.

- *"I do deserve this. But it will require me to step out of my comfort zone and be vulnerable enough to embrace being a beginner."*

- *"It's okay if some people judge me; those aren't the kinds of people I want in my life anyway."*

- *"Who says I can't shine? What evidence do I have to prove that I don't deserve to? I admire other people who shine, so why can't I do the same?"*

- *"I've always been good enough; it's time I start to realize it."*

- *"So what if I fail? Failing is just a redirection, and the true failure is never trying."*

Finally, start paying attention to negative thoughts as they arise in your day-to-day life. Try not to obsess over this. Instead, slowly but surely rewrite the narrative in your head about what you are capable of and what you deserve in life. The reason this is so important is that if you don't believe in yourself, your ideal life will never unfold. Your best and highest self asks you to take a look at your false core beliefs. Next, take the time to rewrite your conditioning. What is the truth about yourself and your capabilities if you examine them through a lens of self-love, grace, and hope? As tedious as this mental rewiring process can be, I promise you, it's worthwhile.

3

The Real Glow Up Is When . . .

You Rewrite the Story You Tell

Yourself in Hardships

We all go through some form of hardship in our lives at varying levels, whether that be the loss of a loved one, a financial hardship, debilitating mental health issues, eating disorders, bodily injuries, emotional abuse, physical abuse, racism, injustice, illness or disease, chronic pain, relationship breakups and heartache, an identity crisis, failed friendships, bullying, natural disasters—you name it. Hardships don't necessarily breed natural inspiration for most people; in fact, it's far easier to shut down in the midst of them. Many find it hard to cope, and those unprocessed and difficult emotions often manifest in other harmful ways, which is *completely* understandable because we are only human and are likely doing the best we can with the tools we have. Let me give you an example: When my father suddenly passed in 2018 after suffering from stage IV melanoma, I was in complete shock and didn't know how to cope with the heavy grief I was experiencing for the very first time. Not only was his loss so jarring, but I experienced added trauma being in the room with him for the two days as he "turned." (This meant his body and mind was beginning to shut down.) As his death was happening in front of my eyes, there was nothing I could do but stay by his side until he finally took his last breath, no matter how uncomfortable and disturbing it felt for me to remain present with him. After his passing, I quickly turned to comfort food and alcohol for solace. Food has been something that has always been a natural go-to for me whenever things feel tough and I want to temporarily escape harsh feelings. I wouldn't say I binged, per se, but in the months following his passing, I did turn to greasy comfort foods in an attempt to numb some of the pain I endured. I'm not talking about the occasional burger or pizza; I'm talking about the haven't-touched-a-vegetable-in-ages eating mindset. I was treating my body like a waste bin. As for drinking, I had already used alcohol as an emotional crutch, if you will. So my nightly wine quickly turned into afternoon wine too. Not to mention the day of my dad's memorial I drank from early morning until night, then followed it by consuming more alcohol the next morning. (I'll be addressing the topic of alcohol more in depth in a later chapter because I think many people struggle with drinking as an escape mechanism.)

My point isn't to induce shame around these methods of coping and numbing. I was surviving the best way I knew how to at the time. However, my point is that hardships can sometimes knock us on our asses. They can disrupt our lives in major ways and make us feel like we are floating through space, trying to survive, clinging to whatever comforts we can find. Relying on maladaptive coping mechanisms on your healing journey might be unavoidable because we all process things in our own way. However, at a certain point, when we start to feel ready, we can choose healthier strategies and we can assign meaning to these events in our lives. Did I feel like it was my dad's time to go? No, of course not. But I did come to understand that he would want nothing more than for me to live a happy and full life. Was I happy the following months after my dad passed? No, I was deeply depressed. It was the first time I had ever fallen victim to this level of depression, and it scared the hell out of me because I didn't know if I'd ever snap out of it. My despair and grief felt like it consumed me and swallowed me whole. But I still knew that at some point I was going to turn my pain into purpose. I knew I was going to use these strong feelings to fuel my desire to truly embrace life. By *embracing life*, I don't mean achieve all the things and be successful in my career. To me, embracing life means to finally get in touch with myself, to feel my pain and hold a gentle space for it, to allow myself to laugh and to play, to find "pockets of joy" in the hard times (as beloved television personality, Jonathan Van Ness often encourages), and to view life's bigger picture with fresh eyes and a new perspective. I now embrace life because I understand that it is a gift we don't know how long will last. I now live boldly with no regrets, as if my life could end at any moment. The silver lining of hardships can "lift the veil," so to speak, allowing us to finally see the bigger picture with more clarity. This is an incredible opportunity to get clear on what you want to learn from a difficult experience so that you can carry its wisdom with you for the rest of your life. Pain is often our greatest teacher.

Feel your pain—all of it. Be compassionate with yourself if you're grasping for unhealthy coping mechanisms. When you are ready and able, please spend some time reflecting on how this hardship can be reframed in a way that helps you to see the beauty in your situation and to restore some hope. How can you turn your pain into purpose?

I'll give you some examples:

- You just went to the doctor for your annual checkup, and your doctor mentions a strong concern with your current weight and/or bloodwork and advises you to consider a major lifestyle change. You are horrified, maybe even filled with shame and embarrassment. (You recognize your habits haven't been very healthy for a while.) You then take some time to process these emotions and eventually decide you are going to turn this into a beautiful, new chapter. You research healthy recipes that make sense for your lifestyle and preferences. You commit to making an effort to focus on moving your body more. You are going to trade your shame for inspiration. This inspiration will be the motivating factor that helps you finally feel your best. Your wake-up call serves as a pivotal point in your health journey, which leads you to feel more energized and, ultimately, to live a healthier life. Without this painful moment, you may have never made these incredible changes for your overall health.

- You're experiencing some intense anxiety and depression and feel overwhelmed by it all. This discomfort and pain leads you to the conclusion that something has to change. You realize that your only option to deal with the issues head-on is to finally get to know where your pain is coming from. This means you will need to talk to a professional. From here, you learn how to be gentle on yourself as you process difficult emotions and memories, and address your triggers along the way. You could have leaned into an addiction or shoved it down more, only to have it reappear as a worse issue later. Instead, you confronted these challenges head-on, found a good therapist, and advocated for your own growth, working toward the happiness and peace you deserve. Your pain and discomfort revealed that you had inner work to do. Your ceiling was the impetus to your healing. Now you feel better than you even knew was possible because you prioritized your mental and emotional well-being in a way you never had before.

- You just got out of a highly toxic relationship, still in disbelief of how you even got to this point and how you tolerated the physical and/or emotional abuse for so long. You feel weak, like you're at your absolute lowest, but you know something has to change. You look back on your dating history and notice all the relationships before this one were toxic in their own way. You feel defeated, unappreciated, and confused. You do some research and realize that although you never deserved this poor treatment, you do have a responsibility to fix this pattern. You realize that for others to love you and treat you well, you need to learn to love and treat yourself well first. You take the time to be alone and heal the parts of you that led you to the wrong people. You learn to set boundaries. You learn to respect yourself. You break a pattern that would have continued for the rest of your life if you didn't have these major realizations birthed by your painful experiences. Your pain was necessary because it showed you there was no other option to stop the cycle except radical self-love and self-discovery. (This scenario can also apply to the friendships in your life.)

Hard moments in life don't have to break you. You can use the experiences to pivot and start fresh. If you need to be a mess for a little bit, do what you need to do and feel your heavy feelings. But please, once you're ready, give yourself the gift of growth and healing. Pain is a powerful teacher; it's worth reflecting on your experiences and examining areas where you can find the beauty and silver lining in it all. (Even if you have to look a little harder.)

Some of the most incredible thought leaders, healers, teachers, artists, and role models have gone through their own tragedies in life, and they had two options: 1) let the pain define them and bitterly ruminate in that pain forever, or 2) feel the pain but then turn it into a life-changing and purposeful moment in their trajectory. If it weren't for painful lessons in my life, I wouldn't have the insight to write this book and help others heal and transform their lives. Did my life feel like a complete mess at times? Absolutely, without a doubt. But there is something to be said of someone who feels their pain, takes the time to process it, makes the necessary changes to heal themselves, and then decides to use that as fuel to help others along the way. It's a beautiful full-circle moment.

Mini Exercise

I want you to think about an obstacle you are currently facing. Something that feels extremely uncomfortable and is tempting to avoid altogether. Once you've thought of that *thing* (or multiple *things*), I want you to acknowledge your pain. Take out your journal, or use your notes app on your phone, and freely write about the pain you are experiencing without the need to correct, dilute, or put it in pretty packaging. Simply focus on getting it all out in the open.

After you've confronted that truth and pain, I want you to use your imagination a little bit. Envision how this painful experience could be transformed into something positive and inspirational for yourself and, eventually, others. (You may have to really dig deep here and take some time to reflect if you're having trouble finding any positive aspects.) The goal of this isn't to rush the process of healing or to deny the pain. The goal of this is to have some hope to refer to on those extra hard days when the pain feels like it's too much to bear.

You may forget what that hope looks like when you're in the midst of deep pain, and that's okay. We are not striving for perfection. We are trying to create an anchor of hope for those dark moments. You would be amazed at how this small shift can aid in carrying you through challenging times. It helps make the messy, healing period feel purposeful.

I recognize your pain may feel like it could swallow you whole some days. I've sat in my own pain, too, where all I had was an inkling of hope to hold onto. It was still uncomfortable at times, but my hope eventually led me down the correct path. No matter how uncomfortable, I still headed in a healthy direction where an eventual light at the end was there to greet me. One day, your strength and your unique story can empower you to inspire someone else. That full-circle moment is what brings meaning to our lives and to our pain.

4

The Real Glow Up Is When . . .

You Allow Yourself to Heal from Trauma

Unresolved trauma can hold us back. The memories that surface can feel overwhelming and larger than life. Some may say "time heals all wounds," and, yes, time is a critical component, but healing doesn't start and end with that simple phrase. Because of the confusing and elusive nature of healing, it can be increasingly tempting to avoid the process altogether, and many people do just that—avoid it. The problem with this method is we rob ourselves of so much when we avoid doing this inner work. The truth is, life can be messy and healing can be messy. And distractions like social media, drugs, alcohol, television, codependency, or a workaholic mindset temporarily allows us to numb our uncomfortable feelings instead of sorting through them. The key word here being *temporary.*

With this approach, you receive a short-term gain in exchange for a long-term struggle. You are unknowingly choosing to carry that unprocessed trauma with you for the rest of your life. The point being, our pain is meant to be felt rather than numbed or ignored. We live in a time that glamorizes "highlight reels," "having it all together," and "pushing through the struggle." We are made to feel weak for being human. But since when is it a weakness to be yourself? To feel your emotions? To me, being myself and feeling my emotions is one of the most natural things I could ever do, but society taught me otherwise. I had to unlearn this habit of shoving my feelings down, and I encourage you to do the same.

I know it doesn't necessarily sound appealing to dive into the challenging aspects of our lives and to sit with the discomfort that arises. In fact, it can be terrifying. That's why perspective is so valuable in this process. You need to remind yourself that you would rather experience temporary compounded pain that comes from healing than to avoid it and experience the long-term, insidious suffering that creeps up on you when you least expect it, negatively influencing the choices you make (without even realizing it). In one sense, unprocessed trauma becomes a weed. It spreads, takes over, and prevents healthy growth. When we choose to tackle these weeds and address them by tending to our gardens, we make room for so much beauty to grow in their place. (For the record, it's never too late to tend to those weeds from your past. It just may require a little extra digging.)

Healing from trauma is brave and requires time and patience. It also requires being extremely gentle with ourselves in the process. On the flip side, it can feel overwhelming, as if you've lost all sense of control. Like you have no choice but to surrender to life and ride out the wave of discomfort. It requires you to hold on to the idea that your temporary struggle will lead to beauty and peace on the other side—if only you can stay true to yourself and *trust the process*, remembering that you need to feel in order to heal.

This healing process can feel like unraveling or breaking and looks different for everyone. For me, it means a lot of resting, removing the pressure to perform, and reminding myself that my worth doesn't come from constantly doing and achieving. Allowing myself to unplug from this idea that I need to always be striving for more, and reminding myself that (although not glamorized, praised, or even noticed) doing this inner work is the path that heeds the most fruitful results in the long-term.

This can all feel complicated to manage, mainly because not many people allow themselves the time to heal. It's a thankless job, even though it's astoundingly beneficial and life-changing. Many choose to avoid the unknown and remain in an illusion of having control. But that's all it is, an illusion, because none of us truly have control. Numbing and shoving down pain or trauma always backfires on us, whether we realize it or not. And since most people don't allow themselves the time and space to do this inner work, they don't know how to talk about it or support your healing journey. It's a foreign concept to so many, and oftentimes just talking about it will feel uncomfortable to other people, which will then make you feel uncomfortable too. This lack of understanding creates pressure from others to be doing more, or to push through things quicker. Their reactions to you can be as simple as a disapproving statement or an awkward look. The secret is to *keep going despite anyone's judgement*. You are not weak for feeling your pain or for creating the space for it to be processed. In fact, you are stronger than most for not numbing or avoiding it.

On my healing journey, it felt notably isolating at times. Feelings are messy, and when people avoid their own mess, they sure as hell don't want to deal with your mess. It's not out of selfishness; it's out of *capacity*. They simply don't have the capacity to hold space for your pain and support your journey. The important thing to remember here is *it's okay*. Judgment or disapproval can feel really scary and even threatening to our safety (as social creatures), but it's okay if people misunderstand you for a little bit. After a while, you can differentiate between the people who are capable of hearing about your process and who are not. With this knowledge, avoid sharing your vulnerable healing journey with those who cannot support you.

It's best to keep the topics light or avoid a particular person altogether if they compromise your growth in any way. This isn't petty; it's the only way to give yourself a fighting chance to heal, *and you deserve to heal.*

This is about you. Only you can advocate for yourself on this journey. In fact, it's often a disservice if you depend on people too much in this process. Yes, healthy and supportive connection can serve as a life raft at this time, but leaning too heavily on someone in your healing process disallows you to find the strength from within to truly grow and evolve in this process. It's really about finding your healthy balance between outward support and inner support. There is so much power in self-love and tending to your pain with self-compassion, so you don't want to miss out on this piece of the puzzle; it's foundational for your personal growth. That being said, on my journey, it would have been a major challenge to heal without the help of a good therapist and/or certain trauma-informed social media accounts that helped guide me through the recovery process and validate my pain when I felt no one else was able to. This piece was so crucial for me. Again, it's all a balancing act.

I want to offer you some advice for how you can tend to your own pain in a way that is simple, yet super effective. When I have a flashback to a painful memory, or if I'm having a tough day where I feel filled with shame and I'm being super hard on myself, I have a go-to practice that has been incredibly beneficial to my healing journey. As mentioned before, we need to "feel to heal," which can be overwhelming and daunting if you don't know what to do with your heavy emotions. When I have big feelings rise up (sometimes seemingly out of nowhere), I like to remind myself to first release all shame and remember that pain is not a weakness, that feelings are not a sign of failure. I then gently place my hand over my chest and speak to myself as I would speak to a child who is experiencing heavy emotions (with a kind, loving approach). First, I validate my pain. For example, I say, "I understand why this past memory (or this tough day) is bringing up sadness or anger for you. It's perfectly normal to feel these emotions." Then I remind myself I am safe. For example: "You are completely safe to feel these big feelings, even if they are overwhelming." Lastly, I say something kind and supportive, such as, "You are doing a beautiful job handling everything. You are so strong." The point of this practice is to create a "safe container" for you to feel these big emotions without shame, guilt, or fear. Oftentimes, we never learned how to properly navigate these emotionally charged situations. Most of us have a tendency to flee, avoid, and then feel shame if we can't escape our discomfort. This is a sure recipe for crippling anxiety and low self-esteem. In essence, through the above practice you are speaking to your "inner child," the part of you that is most vulnerable, who needs your tender care and attention. The part of you who needs endless compassion and reassurance that everything is going to be okay. You can provide that comfort and support for yourself, and that is a beautiful resource to lean on in turbulent times.

A quick reminder to reflect back on the above method:

1) *Release shame.*

2) *Place your hand over your heart.*

3) *Validate your feelings.*

4) *Assure yourself that you are safe to feel every feeling, good or bad.*

5) *Speak positive words of affirmation.*

I think it's also worth noting that emotions, such as anger, can have even more shame tied to them. The truth is, anger gets a bad reputation, but it's a completely normal, healthy emotion to experience. The interesting thing about anger is that it is generally a form of sadness that is linked to your pain. Anger is natural; however, it's important to know how to tend to it so that it does not spill into your relationships or become hurtful and destructive toward those around you. I, for one, have shifted my relationship with anger and have allowed myself the space to feel it when it arises. I like to let it all out in my journal so that I can recognize it, validate it, and then release it. The problem is, when we hold in our frustrations, our issues tend to grow and spread even more. When we acknowledge them without shame, we let these frustrations move through us, allowing us to find peace. We can view anger as a "protective older brother" of sadness. It's often a self-defense toward our hurt feelings. It's meant to protect us, to help us avoid the hurt underneath it all.

I should also mention that at a certain point in your healing journey, you may feel like you've overcome so much, and you're now in an entirely new head space. This is a really empowering place to be; finally feeling safe, whole, and validated. Since healing is not linear, we will have times where we regress for a bit—meaning, something you thought you had moved past completely or let go of will unexpectedly rear its little head back into your life. You may be disappointed that these old feelings seemingly return out of nowhere. You may even be tempted to shove them down and not process them because you thought you had already worked through these issues and healed. Please remember this is completely normal. It is not a reflection of moving backward or failing; it is simply a reminder of how far you've come. Be grateful that these types of feelings don't arise on a regular basis anymore, and approach them with just as much compassion as before. Please don't view this as a step backward. This is natural, and I can speak to it from personal experience. I sometimes will feel so resistant toward letting these feelings in because I fear I'm backsliding into an old pattern. However, as Carl Jung, the well-known Swiss psychologist said, "What you resist not only persists, but will grow in size." No matter how much time has passed, it is just as valuable to acknowledge these feelings as it was in the beginning stages of your journey. This is not an indication of failure. It is natural for emotions to resurface every now and then. Please greet them with love, compassion, and understanding. Try not to overthink why they showed up out of the blue or tie it to your overall progress and fall into a shame spiral. This resurfacing is expected, so allow your emotions to flow in like waves without resisting the current.

Finding the Root

Sometimes diving into your trauma leads to more confusion. Depending on your unique circumstances, you may think, *How did I even get into this situation? Why do I feel this way? How do I break an unhealthy cycle? How do I heal from something so tragic and painful?* Healing sometimes requires you to reflect deeper on the root causes of your pain. I know this can sound overwhelming because it typically means addressing core wounds you have avoided out of self-preservation and survival. However, in order to truly progress and evolve, you need to remain curious about the root causes.

This process often feels like entering into scary territory, especially if you have experienced some major trauma in your life. It's important to be gentle on yourself as you reflect on the possible root causes. Many times, shame accompanies trauma. To replace that shame with self-acceptance and self-compassion is easier said than done. It requires the repetition of disassembling defeating narratives and replacing them with loving truths. This can take time. It can also feel threatening, prompting you to disassociate altogether because the pain is far too much to take in all at once. Whatever this looks like for you, that's okay. Take your time, and please be gentle on yourself. Chances are, if you have deep-rooted pain that has yet to be addressed, there is a reason for it; it's a self-protection mechanism.

This is where the power of a good therapist is often instrumental on your journey. You can do all the soul-searching and reflection you want to, but sometimes you're going to hit a wall. You can't always navigate trauma on your own; sometimes you need the support and guidance of a licensed professional to walk you through it—if you have the means and resources to access one, of course. (I'll be sure to provide some helpful suggestions in this chapter if going to a therapist isn't financially feasible for you at this time, because for so many it unfortunately is not.)

On the flip side, sometimes seeing a professional is terrifying. Even though you are supported, you are still navigating deep, buried pain. Will you do me a favor? Keep going anyway. Feel the fear and persist. You may feel intense resistance, but it's often your mind's way of trying to protect you. However, trust me when I say that your brain is an incredible organ. You can and you will metabolize this pain over time, but the only way out is through. Again, *you must feel to heal*. You must know the difference between perceived danger and real danger. Sometimes digging up old trauma can feel like real danger. Please be gentle on yourself if this happens, but keep showing up and doing the work anyway. Our brain can heal and be renewed. We can create new neural pathways over time (with patience). We are not destined to live in pain forever. We have the ability to heal and create new ways of being.

It's also important to mention that not all therapists are going to be a good fit for you. So it's important to listen to your gut if something about your connection feels off, or if they have a habit of misunderstanding you. If you already have trouble trusting yourself, it's imperative to find a therapist you can trust. At the end of the day, therapists are humans, with their own issues and insecurities, and some of them will display unhealthy tendencies or cross boundaries. You should educate yourself on what is considered healthy in a client-patient dynamic so you have something to reference going into it. I don't say this to scare you out of seeking therapy. My goal is to train you to trust your instincts and be brave enough to end therapy relationships no matter what stage they are in, if you feel they are incompatible or if they make you feel emotionally unsafe. There are many wonderful, kind, and compassionate therapists out there, but you just need to trust your gut instinct if it doesn't feel like a good fit, and bow out with grace. You can always end the relationship via email if it feels uncomfortable. You don't need to explain why. You can simply say, "Thank you for your time. However, I don't think this is a good fit for me." That's it. That's an adequate reason. Please be patient enough to find the right therapist. I promise it is worth it, and I promise you deserve it.

As mentioned above, therapy is not always affordable or accessible to everyone. I find this unbelievably disappointing because I think all people should be entitled to professional mental health support regardless of their financial standing. Let me provide some advice and alternative methods for obtaining support if you're lacking resources right now. (Because your mental health journey matters just as much as anyone else's.) To start, you can look into federally qualified health care centers and see what they might offer you. You can also research and see if you qualify for free therapy through Medicaid. Additionally, something that worked well for me, and was very beneficial, was to find a third-party nonprofit, such as Open Path Collective, to get approved for therapy at a more affordable out-of-pocket rate. For community resources, most cities offer free support groups tailored to fit various needs and issues. For additional guidance (not therapy), you can self-educate and subscribe to credible podcasts and YouTube channels created by licensed therapists, you can seek out relevant self-help books, or follow trauma-informed social media accounts. (Please trust your gut with social media accounts just like you would a therapist. If something feels off, trust that instinct and move along. There are plenty of other resources available to you.)

It can sometimes take months before you are able to see a professional. This often feels incredibly disheartening, and I have experienced this issue myself. Please try to remain hopeful and be creative in pursuing free resources, support groups, journaling practices, and perhaps confiding in someone close to you that you know you can trust to be a compassionate listener. It's important to work with whatever resources you have. However, if you are feeling suicidal, please be sure to call a trusted suicide prevention hotline ASAP.

Healing the Root

Talk therapy—with a well-matched, trusted therapist—is a surefire way to begin healing the root of your trauma. Additionally, there are other healing modalities beyond talk therapy that you could benefit from. For example, somatic healing is focused around the mind-body connection. Some examples of somatic healing include: Reiki, EMDR, massage, yoga, breathing techniques, dance therapy, meditation, neurofeedback therapy, and acupuncture. The school of thought behind these modalities is that trauma is stored in the body and can manifest in harmful ways (such as illness) if not addressed. I highly recommend the book *The Body Keeps the Score: Brain, Mind, and Body in the Healing of Trauma* by Bessel Van Der Kolk. He shares how the mind and body are connected, going into detail about various healing methods. I was inspired by his teachings to look into neurofeedback therapy, a noninvasive treatment that encourages the brain to develop healthier patterns of activity. Through this training, your brain creates new and healthier neural pathways, allowing you to reduce symptoms of anxiety and depression, improve attention and focus, increase emotional stability, and treat PTSD symptoms. Last summer I visited a neurofeedback therapy clinic on a weekly basis (I did my research and found a credible physician in this field). This treatment was life-changing for me on my healing journey, and I instantly experienced the benefits just after a couple of sessions. I was less anxious, and my brain was no longer defaulting to a state of fight-or-flight anymore. Through this treatment, I was able to be more spontaneous, remain calm under pressure, and tap into my creative side with greater ease. The effects of this therapy are lifelong after attending approximately ten to twenty sessions (the number of sessions will vary person to person). The treatment itself is very quick, and I found each session to be quite relaxing. I share this example to demonstrate that there are many methods of healing that can help you in your journey, so it's best to keep an open mind along the way.

Mini Exercise

Do you suffer from feelings of anxiety? Anxiety is scary and is highly prevalent these days. As a result, the stigma around it is lessening, allowing more sufferers to openly seek help. I challenge you to reflect on what makes you anxious. In what situations do you find yourself triggered to feel it the most? (This could be related to a deeper trauma.) Is it in social situations? Around certain people? When you feel like you lack control over a situation? When you are not constantly *doing* and *striving*? When you are experiencing a health issue? A finance issue? I encourage you to pick one or two scenarios and journal about what causes you anxiety in that situation, then take the time to dive a little deeper into why you might be experiencing this.

For example, let's say you have social anxiety. Do you struggle with feeling comfortable in your own skin? Do you have a fear of rejection? Or have you been betrayed before so it feels scary to put yourself out there and be vulnerable? Let's say it's the first scenario: you don't feel comfortable in your own skin. Let's try to go a little deeper. When in your life did you first start to feel this way? As a child? Grade school? After an abusive relationship that taught you to doubt yourself? These are the teachable moments for you to reflect on and begin your healing journey. Take small steps, reflect, identify, and then create a new story for yourself. Speak to yourself in these moments as you would a best friend. Write yourself a loving and supportive letter, and include everything you know you need to hear right now.

Here's an example:

I see why social interactions make you freeze up and not feel safe. You were bullied as a kid, and this shaped your perception of yourself. That was a really painful experience, and that pain has stuck with you. But you are an incredible person, and your bullying experiences said nothing about you and everything about them. You were always loveable, good enough, and you've always had so much to offer. It may take some time to fully believe that, but people are lucky to have you contribute to conversations and to show up. You are safe to be yourself now and open up to new people. Try to be gentle on yourself as you remind yourself of these truths. It may take some time, and there may be growing pains, but you got this! I believe in you. Remember: you are loveable and the world needs people like you.

5

The Real Glow Up Is When . . .

You Regularly Practice Self-Care

I was so used to not making time for my self-care needs that when I finally did, I felt strangely selfish and even guilty about it. Hopefully, you don't struggle with that same feeling, but if you do, I understand. No matter what, you completely deserve every ounce of self-care, even if that takes some time for you to truly accept, or if it's something you have to remind yourself of. My self-care routine used to consist of the occasional face mask and Netflix binge. (Full disclaimer: still fully love both of those things, but I needed more than just that.) I needed to go a little deeper if I wanted to prioritize my mental health and tend to my personal needs.

If showing up for yourself feels like a challenge, you can start by viewing this through a different lens. Oftentimes, we find it much easier to show up for others, or let's say a child within our care, but when it comes to ourselves, this level of care can be overlooked entirely. We've become so accustomed to just "pushing through it," as if it's a valiant, selfless act, but it's not. Denying our needs is a form of self-neglect. If you relate to this, I urge you to view self-care as an act of love for your inner child. We all have an inner child, and when we take care of ourselves, they feel safe, seen, and loved. Be the adult in your life who creates a healthy environment for yourself. Give your inner child the gift of stability and love until it feels more natural for you; because when you care for them, you are really caring for yourself. It's all relevant. It's simply a different way of looking at things.

Life is a journey, and in order to survive it and enjoy it, we require special care and attention. We are complex beings with various needs, whether they be emotional, mental, spiritual, physical, relational, financial, or spatial. When we ignore these needs, we suffer. For example, when we hyperextend ourselves without adequate rest and downtime, we trigger our *sympathetic* nervous system (in other words, we begin to operate from a state of fight-or-flight, alerting our body to think we are in danger), causing extreme anxiety, increased reactivity (anger), illness, and ultimately leading us to burnout. However, when we make the special effort to care for ourselves and rest when our body calls for it—go on walks, spend time in nature, practice deep breathing, process emotions through journaling, crack open a book, take a bath or shower—we activate our *parasympathetic* nervous system, sending signals to our body that we are safe, allowing us to lower our heart rate, experience healthy digestion, and operate from a state of peace with a clear and calm mind. This world is fast-paced, and we often try to spread ourselves thin in order to meet the demands and expectations set by society. But there is a reason why anxiety and depression are so prevalent and why, for example, autoimmune illnesses are increasing. We may not be able to change the societal norms, but we can certainly advocate for our own well-being in this lifetime. I will add, this isn't to say you won't ever experience anxiety or depression again, but this is certainly one crucial piece of the mental health puzzle that is deserving of your attention. Changing how we see the world, and how we operate within it, is no easy feat. Remaining in your parasympathetic nervous system is a delicate dance, and it's completely normal to stumble, or mis a step along the way. What's important is that you gently remind yourself to practice the necessary self-care to get back into it. We are humans with messy lives, and different seasons of life will require different levels of energy and grit. Regardless, you can be intentional and focus on these basic tenets of self-care to enhance your physical and mental well-being, allowing you to feel safer in your mind, body, and in the world around you. You deserve to feel safe and secure.

Below are the self-care techniques that help me feel the most grounded.

Journaling

Journaling was, and still is, such a pivotal tool in my self-care routine. It all started when a therapist recommended it in one of our sessions, and I'm so grateful she did. My favorite style of journaling is a "brain dump," which is the process of filling up one to three pages (or however many you need) of whatever is on your mind or the various emotions you are feeling—completely unfiltered. No need to read it back. Simply release your thoughts and leave it be. This practice has been life-changing for me, especially at a time where I felt fairly isolated, broken down, and confused. I learned I didn't necessarily need someone to vent all my problems to. I realized I could actually take matters into my own hands. Plus, with a brain-dump journal practice, chances are there may be some things you wouldn't want to share with a friend anyway. This free-flow writing exercise allows you to be ultra-vulnerable and unfiltered with your thoughts, without the need to sugarcoat them.

I've found there is so much beauty in this process. I instantly feel lighter when I let go of my messy thoughts and feelings; it's as if I'm untangling my mind. It's calming knowing I have this space I can hold for myself. A safe place where I can purge all my wild insecurities, express anger, express sadness, express confusion, and, eventually, express gratitude and joy for how far I've come and where I'm at now. Journaling feels like I've finally found a place that allows me to stop hiding, a place where I can unapologetically be *me*. This has not only helped me to feel more in tune with my feelings, but it has enabled me to accurately assess my needs with regard to self-care. The beauty is, we have this power within and don't need to depend on someone else to receive this major sense of relief and support. There is something to be said of just getting your thoughts out and bringing them to the surface instead of shoving them deep down. You begin to release the invisible weight that has been limiting you for far too long.

When we pretend things are good all the time without making the space to process the sadness and anger that inevitably pops up in our lives, we are unknowingly manifesting more anxiety and pain for ourselves. It may feel okay for now, but trust me when I say we all have a breaking point. This avoidance method only works for so long before the pendulum inevitably swings, and we're then found swimming in our pain and discomfort that we deliberately tried to avoid for so long. This pain inside of us is begging to be seen and metabolized.

Expressing anger and sadness when it hit, rather than bottling it up, was a huge growth point for me. My whole life I had thought messy emotions were bad and something to feel shameful about. I have since learned that's the furthest thing from the truth. Humans feel emotions—it's a natural part of life. How could something unavoidable be deemed as bad or shameful? The truth is, many people are burying their emotions; they avoid, they numb, and they can't bear the idea of directly facing the uncomfortable feelings that arise. This was me too. I'm here to say that if I've just described you, I fully understand and empathize. Oftentimes, society encourages an unhealthy mentality: "Work hard. Be happy. Push through it. Good vibes only." I prefer the authentic, compassionate, more sustainable one: "Feel your messy feelings. Show yourself compassion. Let those feelings go. And feel way lighter and healthier by doing so."

In terms of how you choose to journal, there are many studies detailing the wonderful advantages of writing pen to paper versus typing on a device. For example, the process is more intimate; the brain connects differently, and creativity is sparked in new ways. Plus, it's said to be more therapeutic. If you have fears about someone finding your most intimate thoughts, invest in a miniature shredder, and shred each page when you're done. Or find a journal lock box, and tuck it away somewhere private when you're finished. Most importantly, please don't rob yourself of this beautiful and intimate experience. The privacy issue was a fear I had to work through, and I'm so grateful I have.

Disclaimer: If you discover journaling isn't for you, I hope you still allow yourself to sit with and feel your feelings (even the messy and tough ones that bring up shame or discomfort). I know it can sometimes feel like the dragging weight of these emotions will never go away, but if you offer yourself space for your feelings to be seen and felt, they will eventually dissipate. However, when we avoid uncomfortable feelings, or invalidate them, we are essentially letting those feelings run on a loop where they have nowhere productive to go (often leading us to feel more anxious).

A Hot Bath (or Shower)

Baths have been so soothing for my nervous system, especially after a challenging day. I really only dedicate twenty or thirty minutes to them, which absolutely does the trick because eventually you begin to feel the "hot-tub effect" and want to get out and feel the cold air again. These baths are like a magical reset button for me. They help to let go of the tension of the day, and I feel safe, warm, and completely at ease in my body. If you are thinking, *I don't like baths*, I urge you to give one a try and see what your perfect bath would consist of. Maybe you hang fresh eucalyptus from the shower head and bask in the natural aroma. Maybe you pour in Epsom salts and add a few drops of your favorite essential oil to further promote physical relaxation. Some prefer to shower first, feeling nice and clean when stepping in, or maybe you'll enjoy a shower afterward to clean off. It's all about what feels best for you. But I challenge you to give it a try. It's possible that you just haven't figured out your ideal bath scenario.

For those who swear off all baths despite my hard-sell, a hot shower can be just as relaxing to your nervous system (and perhaps better suited to your busy schedule). You can still cultivate a calming experience by putting a few drops of an essential oil in each corner of the shower and playing therapeutic music, creating a spa-like feeling. Connecting with your body through the physical comfort that hot water can provide is both a healing and grounding exercise.

Essential Oils

I use essential oils in various ways. For example, I use my peppermint oil roller for tension headaches by applying it to my temples, the nape of my neck, and behind my ears, then massage it in. I experience a nice cooling effect, and it provides instant relief that generally lasts about an hour. I also use the peppermint roller for therapeutic purposes. Rolling it on the side of my hand and inhaling a few breaths invigorates me while also providing a (scientifically) tranquilizing effect on my brain, which helps me if I'm feeling stressed. Something about inhaling this fresh, sharp scent brings me back into the present moment and comforts me. This is especially helpful when at an event or when travelling.

There are many ways to use essential oils. In my case, it's about finding my favorite calming scents and incorporating them into my day where I know they'd best suit me. It's something I don't have to think about in much detail. For example, I keep my peppermint roller in my purse or on my bedside table. My lavender oil dropper stays on the counter next to my shower. My eucalyptus oil sits on the ledge of my bathtub—and that's it! I will sometimes use an essential oil diffuser, but not regularly (because I often forget to fill it and use it). However, I know many people find the diffusers to be therapeutic as well. In my opinion, essential oils can be a built-in, low-fuss self-care practice that's helpful if you want to feel pampered and comforted. You can think of it as aromatherapy.

Guided Meditations

You may have heard about the seemingly endless benefits of mediation: reduced stress and anxiety, increased emotional health, enhanced self-awareness, lengthened attention span, increased kindness and empathy, better overall sleep, reduction in physical pain, decreased blood pressure—the list goes on and on. Sounds pretty great, right? There are various methods of meditation, but I personally find the guided meditations to be the most beginner friendly. The challenge is that our "thinking minds" are accustomed to running the show, and it can be difficult to let go of all our thoughts and embrace this mindful practice. (Which is why it's a practice, because no meditation is perfect.)

There are various ways to get into a meditative state. Some choose exercise, creating art, writing, or cooking, basically any activity that allows a person to be in the present moment instead of obsessing over to-do lists or current troubles. For me, I've found that guided meditations work well with my lifestyle. There are plenty of apps, streaming services, or even free YouTube videos to try if you're on a budget. My favorite part is the ability to custom pick what type of meditation I want to listen to, depending on what I feel I need most that day. In your search you can choose to be ultra specific, or you can be as vague as you want. I typically reserve about ten minutes at night to plug in my headphones and meditate before I fall asleep. This helps me tune into myself and let go of the day rather than ruminate on what could have been done better. Another time I find these guided meditations useful is first thing in the morning. It's a great way to set a positive, peaceful tone for the day and to take time for your self-care. Guided meditations are available whenever and wherever you deem appropriate. Hopping on a flight, a quick break from work in your car, or before a big presentation or networking event. You can obviously choose which moments are most beneficial to you, such as when you need some perspective and peace, or to simply ground yourself in the moment. Meditation is an incredible tool at your disposal, and it's no doubt been helpful in my self-care routine.

Disclaimer: It can be difficult to shut off the mind during meditation. This is a normal experience for people. It's important to not get frustrated about this. The more sessions you practice, the less your mind will interrupt you. Regardless of whether your thoughts interrupt your mediation, you're still much better off showing up and doing it than avoiding meditation all together. You will still experience positive results either way. Please don't be too hard on yourself or cheat yourself from all of these benefits due to a fear of imperfection.

Supplements

I was hesitant to include this topic because I am not a doctor or a professional qualified to talk to you about supplements. However, I'd be lying if I didn't mention the role they play within my self-care routine. I will preface this section by saying that you should always do your own research and talk to your doctor to make sure these supplements are a good fit for you. For example, some supplements may not be allowed if you are already taking a medication that could interfere with it and cause issues. So please do your due diligence.

I never took supplements until recent years (unless you count a Flintstones multivitamin), so this was a whole new world for me. Last year, I had a naturopathic physician suggest a few supplement options, and they have played a helpful role in my mental health. To start, I take an adaptogen every morning called ashwagandha; it helps me cope with anxiety and helps to reduce the level of cortisol in my body (a stress hormone). Every night I take a magnesium chelate powder by mixing a small scoop of into a glass of warm water. It is known to help your body relax, and it's also been said to provide adequate nutrition to support the health of the brain. My naturopathic physician mentioned it's common for us to be deficient in magnesium, which is why it's good for brain health. I struggle with mild depression occasionally, and I've found that taking 5-HTP (on the days I'm experiencing depression symptoms) is helpful for raising serotonin levels in my brain. These three supplements have become a big part of my self-care routine, and I'm so grateful I discovered them. If you're interested in any of these, please speak to a healthcare professional to see if they are a good fit for you. I've recently learned that there is nothing to be ashamed of in needing a little help from supplements. I used to think it was high maintenance, but I now know it's a form of self-care; and we deserve that level of care.

Unplugging

This one's big, especially in such a digitally focused world. We are constantly looking at screens—work, email, TV, streaming services, and the big one . . . social media. We aren't designed to be constantly hunched over, looking at a device. We need to be thoughtful and intentional about creating a balance. One way I do this is by reaching for a book when I'm feeling a little overstimulated by screens but still looking for a form of entertainment. Reading is an activity that I always feel good about because it's calming and grounding, as opposed to social media, where it's so easy to get sucked into mindless scrolling or inundated with tragic or scary news. Our brains weren't designed to compute so much information at once; it's just not healthy, and it's no wonder anxiety is so prevalent these days. I've found that when life feels super overwhelming or challenging, I need to take a day off from social media (and sometimes a week). It's typically most challenging during these hard times because we are so used to reaching for our phone out of distraction. It serves as a mini escape, so to speak. However, I've also learned that my mental health benefits the most when I'm able to flex self-restraint. If that's too hard for you because of work, maybe you could set a strict time limit for yourself so you aren't mindlessly scrolling several times a day. I get it. It can definitely be an obstacle, especially when it's such an ingrained habit. Something that is helpful for me is to move the social media apps I typically use to a random folder on my phone. The reason for this? It's so habitual for us, that we often open the apps on complete autopilot when no conscious decision was even made. Further proof of this for me was when I did move my apps to a separate folder, I found myself opening up the apps that were now taking the place of where the social media apps used to be. I realized that most of the times I'm on these apps, I didn't even consciously choose to open them in the first place. My habits just blindly took me there. What's scarier is how much time we spend on them from a seemingly "blind decision."

Don't get me wrong. Social media can certainly be an empowering and fun place, and I'm in no way here to bash it. However, I do think our mental health can benefit from some thoughtful moderation. Earlier this year, I found myself in a funk, and social media felt like a scary place for me because I was often falling prey to the comparison trap and feeling like I wasn't good enough or doing enough. I made the decision to take one week off from social media. I allowed myself to go on Pinterest (since that typically relaxes and inspires me), but Instagram, TikTok, and Facebook were neatly tucked away in a folder and were off-limits. I held back from the temptation to open them. By the end of the week, I was in such a better space mentally. I felt calm, centered, and less pressured to "have it all figured out." I felt like I could finally hear my thoughts better and breath deeper. I was free to relax and take time for myself without outside narratives bleeding in. Whatever your social media tendencies are, I encourage you to pay attention to how you're feeling, especially if you aren't in a good space mentally. None of us were given manuals for social media as it's a relatively new invention. But we can take it upon ourselves to set healthy boundaries with these habits. Which leads me to the next section . . .

Social Media Boundaries

This section pairs well with the above advice but dives a little deeper into how we can create an online space that feels safe, beneficial, and kind to ourselves. You have control over who you follow, and you are not obligated to follow anyone who makes you feel bad about yourself or stressed out. My social media feeds used to be all over the place. I followed celebrities because I thought I was "supposed to," without any genuine connection to the type of content they would post. It was a space where I tried desperately to keep up with what was "new" and "trendy." One day I realized this wasn't working for me anymore. My feed wasn't a space that felt like it was mine. I spent time unfollowing anyone who I didn't feel was serving my best interest (accounts I didn't feel connected with). Additionally, I've made an effort to seek out the accounts that feel in line with who I am and make me feel good. This wasn't necessarily an "all at once" scenario. I allowed myself the time to simply start paying attention and reflect on these questions: "Why am I following this person? Does this content resonate with me or make me feel good?" I then would kindly unfollow (depending on the varying answers). The beauty is that you don't have to follow anyone; it is your curated space. Please, by all means give yourself permission to choose who you want to follow, and if it's a sticky situation and you feel like you may offend the person (if it's a coworker, friend, or family member), you can simply use the "mute" features. As of now, I follow people who I look up to, who I care about, who live the kind of life I admire, who are encouraging, and who are using their platforms to be honest and vulnerable in a way that makes me feel connected to them. Self-care requires you to follow people and accounts that make you feel good (and depending on where you are in life, those may be subject to change, and that's okay).

Disclaimer: This doesn't necessarily mean unfollow any account that challenges you to think differently, but it does mean following accounts that are aligned with your life, your goals, and how you want to show up in this world. Only you can determine that balance, and it's totally within your rights to do so. This is about creating a safer space to scroll.

Time in Nature

I've learned over the past few years how the simple act of stepping outside and breathing in some fresh air for five to ten minutes instantly calms my nervous system. The American Psychological Association says, "Spending time in nature is linked to both cognitive benefits and improvements in mood, mental health and emotional well-being. Feeling connected to nature can produce similar benefits to well-being, regardless of how much time one spends outdoors." It's easy to feel disconnected to the earth we live on. We often get so caught up in all that's materialistic and superficial. To restore this balance, try to make a special effort to get outside when you're feeling overwhelmed or overstimulated (bonus points if you can make it a part of your routine before you get to that point). Nature is a gift. Never underestimate the healing benefits of going outside and looking up at a sunset-painted sky or a clear, starry night, listening to the birds chirp, walking through a quiet forest, or planting your bare feet in the soft grass. Nature is healing.

Rest

We are conditioned to work hard at all costs and to sacrifice rest for productivity. The trouble is, the cost is dire. The cost is your mental and physical health, your mood, your stress levels, your immune system, your metabolism, your nervous system, and your ability to focus. Rest is an essential part of life, yet it's rarely encouraged. Some cultures understand its importance. For example, in Italy, they are known to take a *riposo*, respectively meaning "extended midday break" where shops tend to close for ninety minutes to two hours each day, allowing workers to go home, take a long lunch or even nap. I don't know about you, but I grew up in a culture and society where rest was not prioritized; in fact, I learned to equate rest as a synonym for being lazy.

Making time to rest in a busy world is a radical act of self-care. Making time to rest in a culture that frowns upon it is brave. We must be brave if we want to adequately take care of ourselves. We need to advocate for our needs regardless of what the norm is. We need to trade in *hustle culture* for *rest culture*. This isn't to say we don't have goals or that we aren't hard workers. What is crucial is to know the importance of both, and to know that our work flourishes when we are able to balance the two. You shouldn't have to sacrifice your overall health for your goals. This is no way to live.

If you are anything like me, rest doesn't come easy. I've battled with feeling guilty when I rest by thinking of myself as lazy by doing so. It's something I actively work to reprogram in my mind because I now know that rest is an essential part of life, and it's nothing to be ashamed of. I share this because you may experience some resistance around rest, too, if you've been conditioned to feel inadequate when doing so. Give yourself grace as you learn to incorporate and weave in restful moments into your life. You may experience resistance, but that's not a reflection of it being bad; it's a reflection of what society has taught you your whole life. You deserve rest. You shouldn't have to save it for when burnout or illness strikes. In fact, the more you incorporate rest throughout the day, the less chance you have of burnout and illness occurring. Rest can be a preventative measure rather than a remedy. You can learn to lean into it, to enjoy it, to cherish it. Rest is self-care, and I hope you give yourself that care you so deeply deserve.

Disclaimer: We all come from different circumstances, work environments, and socioeconomic backgrounds. Rest may be more of a challenge for you to implement than just the mental resistance around it. You may find it less realistic due to your need to pay bills, care for others, and/or survive. I want to be sensitive and empathize with these instances too. However, if it's at all within your capabilities to incorporate a little rest, I highly encourage you to make time for it. These small efforts will give you the strength and good health you need to carry on.

Going for a Walk

If you're able to, another way to incorporate nature into your life is to go on a walk. Walking provides a host of mental health benefits, aiding in stress management, clearing brain fog, boosting creativity, releasing endorphins, enhancing problem-solving skills, and increasing self-esteem (to name a few). You don't need to walk for miles to accomplish this either, according to the Anxiety and Depression Association of America, a simple ten-minute walk may be as effective as a forty-five-minute workout in terms of reducing anxiety and depression. If you can build a short walk into your day, you are caring for your mental health in extraordinary ways.

Making Time to Play

It's so easy to get caught up with to-dos and goal check points that we forget life is supposed to be lived in the midst of all this leveling up. Without this balance, you're not only cheating yourself and your quality of life, but you're actually jeopardizing your ability to reach your fullest potential. You see, some of the best ideas come to you after a week of rest, a fun trip, or a long, playful weekend. The brain cannot function at its highest capacity when it's always in go-mode; it needs time to decompress. And as great as it is to have long-term goals and plans, we need to be able to find joy in the present moment as we strive for more. When you're chasing your dreams, you're in this for the long haul. It can be easy to get tunnel vision and only see our goals and never-ending to-do lists. Sometimes you need to remind yourself to lighten up (I know I do). It may take some time to find the right balance for you, but I guarantee this is another secret to your success. So the next time you are irritable, fatigued, lacking creativity, impatient, or uninspired, ask yourself, *When was the last time I did something fun, relaxing, or spontaneous?* When you get really good at this, you'll find ways to incorporate fun throughout your day-to-day life. And if you feel stressed about lack of money or time, or feel like you don't have enough friends, I promise you there are things you can do to create pockets of fun in your life. You may just need to be a little more creative along the way. Making time for play is a form of self-care.

Mini Exercise

Did any of the above self-care techniques sound appealing to you? If so, give yourself the gift of implementing some (or all) of these habits. I think what's most important here is giving yourself permission to practice self-care. Take some time and brainstorm what sounds best suited for you and your current lifestyle. How can you realistically implement them into your life? It's okay to start small. In fact, it's often the simple practices that heed the biggest results anyway. You don't need to spend a bunch of money to show up for yourself. For example, you have the breath in your lungs and the choice to intentionally take deeper inhales and longer exhales. You have access to books and the ability to put your phone down for a bit. You can step outside and spend time in nature throughout your day. You can grab a sheet of paper and a pen and write down how you're feeling. Remember, it's best to not overcomplicate things. Luckily, the more you make time for these grounding self-care techniques, the more habitual they become. Remember, this isn't self-indulgent behavior; it's called taking care of yourself so you can show up as your best self in life. Everyone benefits from your self-care in the long run, making it a selfless act.

6

The Real Glow Up Is When . . .

You Are Surrounded by a Supportive Inner Circle

Your inner circle is crucial to your overall happiness and success. Depending on the health of your current friendships, you may need to reassess where people stand in your life. Simply put, the people in your circle are either draining your positive energy or contributing to it. This one took me forever to realize, but I'm certainly glad I did. It was a slow (and sometimes tedious) process to filter out certain relationships in my life, but it put me on such a beautiful course to self-love and growth. There is no way around this step. You may think you can overcompensate on your end to try and make something work, but that's the whole point of this lesson. Trying harder to make an imbalanced, toxic relationship work is a waste of your precious energy. A relationship should be fifty-fifty, not seventy-five/twenty-five. Chances are, if you are the one trying harder to make something work, it's because the other person isn't carrying their end of the weight.

Many people don't even know what a healthy relationship or friendship looks like, and this creates a pattern of disappointment and confusion without even realizing we are tolerating less than we deserve. So let's go over the basics. What does a healthy relationship look and feel like?

- Mutual respect for one another. (Be honest and set boundaries comfortably without silent treatments, frequent tension, or arguments.)
- Open and honest communication. (Communicate feelings respectfully. Trust in the other person.)
- Autonomy (Maintain individuality and support each other's separate interests.)
- Compromise (One person can't always get their way.)
- Emotional regulation. (Learn healthy forms of anger management, such as deep breaths and taking time or space before responding when upset.)
- Empathy and support. (Take time to put yourself in your partner's shoes and respond with compassion. Hold space for each other in turbulent times.)
- Self-confidence. (A confident friend or partner is able to love themselves, resulting in a beautifully well-balanced relationship where your success or other friendships don't provoke jealousy or bitterness.)
- Accountability for actions. (Humility and admitting when you are wrong promotes trust and fosters authentic connection.)

To elaborate on the above list, there is a consistency factor here that's profoundly important. Oftentimes, in toxic relationships you may receive the above *some of the time*, and that's a major red flag. Be wary of those who tend to oscillate from *hot to cold*. Another factor is accountability, which some people avoid at all costs. You'll want to limit your interactions with those people if you can. That being said, there is another category of behavior where they *do* take accountability and frequently apologize, yet they fail to make the necessary and consistent changes that are in line with their apology. It's in your best interest to avoid these people too.

Something I had to finally learn the hard way is that not all people are capable of change. For the caring and considerate relationship and friendship idealists out there (believe me, I once was one myself), the people around you would have to *want to change* for there to even be a fighting shot at improving the relationship. This is when you truly pay attention to see if their words line up with their actions. Some have mastered the art of pretending to work on something in order to convince you to move on and forget, but then they have no consistent execution or follow-up on their end. Trust me when I say, this is a form of manipulation. I know this can all sound a little dark or pessimistic, but who you allow in your inner circle is crucial to your long-term happiness and success. I had to learn these lessons the hard way. I had to experience pain in many relationships (friendship, and otherwise) before I realized I'm the one in control of my circumstances, and I can choose how I let people treat me. This inspired my research and understanding of what's healthy versus what is harmful in relationships. What I had thought was acceptable was far from it. I needed to redefine my expectations and standards. Something that genuinely stuck with me and helped me to simplify all of this was to learn to trust my gut instinct. If a connection feels off but you can't exactly place your finger on why it feels that way, you already know more about this relationship than you think. Our nervous systems can pick up on what is safe versus what is harmful. Our bodies know what energy is healthy for us. Pay attention to how you feel around certain people, and limit your exposure to them if they instill negative feelings in you. It doesn't mean you can't love them from a distance; it means you are protecting your precious energy.

You may be thinking, *There are so many people in my life that match this description of a harmful relationship . . . so am I just supposed to be alone all the time?* This question is a little tough. Why? Because oftentimes, if you attract people who tend to take advantage of you or who don't seem to appreciate you or respect you, then toxic relationships could be all you know at this point. It could be your normal. You want the hard truth? Please begin to create space between you and them. But here's another helpful tip that may bring you comfort: oftentimes, if you begin the practice of politely speaking up for yourself, setting healthy boundaries, investing time in your own unique interests, and taking the time to love yourself and practice self-care, you'll begin to notice these "not so healthy" friendships or relationships disappear and dissolve on their own. The reason they disappear? They profited (so to speak) off your lack of self-worth and self-respect. People who genuinely care about you would be so happy for your growth, maybe even inspired by it. People who distance themselves or create conflict to try and make you feel guilty for these positive changes? *They* are not your people. Unfortunately, they don't care about you; instead, they care about what you can do for them. Now does this hurt? Absolutely, this process is painful to realize if you've poured out so much love and respect for someone who ultimately wanted nothing more than to walk all over you and use you. It's extremely hurtful no matter how you look at it. Allow yourself to feel that pain so you can begin healing and empowering yourself to eventually create an inner circle of people who love, respect, and support you.

After this realization, my circle of friends dwindled down to almost nothing. It was such a strange and lonely feeling. I had always been surrounded by many people, so the vacancy felt uncomfortable to me. I knew it was crucial to not automatically run to new, unhealthy friendships in order to fill the void of the previous ones. I knew I was partially responsible for allowing this pattern to continue, and I had to do my part to break the cycle once and for all. What did this mean for me? It meant I had to focus on self-love, self-care, self-respect, and being extremely picky about what relationships feel mutual and healthy. I can honestly say that having a few, or possibly no, friends in this time of transformation is more beneficial than having a group of friends who are secretly "drilling holes in your boat" while you are rowing.

This oftentimes brings up challenging emotions, especially in a time where social media is so prevalent. You may see others posting about their beloved friend groups, or their "best friends forever," and truthfully, this can all sting a bit if you're in this phase of being alone. But it's okay. Let it sting at first. Some people are fortunate enough to have these beautiful and healthy relationships surrounding them, and you can choose to let it inspire hope for your future friendships. However, many (more than you realize) are wrapped up in unhealthy friend-group dynamics and only share a neatly crafted image on social media. Most people don't want to air the grievances of their friend issues online. They aren't going to post a beautifully well-posed photo with the caption: "Ashley was in a miserable mood this whole trip because she missed her boyfriend. And Beth got too drunk and screamed at me for no apparent reason one night and never apologized. Also, I felt pretty left out at times. I wish this trip had gone more smoothly." Not a chance this caption would be posted. You are more likely to read something like: "Such a beautiful trip with the most amazing friends I could ever ask for!" The intent here is not to shame people for sugarcoating experiences on social media. I have certainly been guilty of this too. The purpose of shedding light on the false joy many people post is to remind you that not everything is as it seems when scrolling and comparing your life to another's on social media. The more often you can remind yourself of this, the less often it will hurt, especially if you're intentionally taking the time to distance yourself from people while you learn to cultivate more self-love, respect, and healthy boundaries.

One more thing to be wary of are people who want to rush relationships from the very start: expecting to see you all the time, giving constant (and excessive) compliments, jumping to labels too soon (such as "in a relationship," "soul mates," "best friends," "in love," or "twin flames") without knowing you very long. Basically, be wary of someone who gives you the feeling of "wow, this is almost too good to be true." If you're lonely or craving more connection, these labels could definitely be appealing to you. The issue with this is that healthy relationships allow for autonomy and authenticity and require some time to build trust in a natural way that flows. Super-rushed relationships are generally a red flag and usually end up representing the type of person who runs hot and cold, is untrustworthy, and ends up treating you differently once their "mask" slips a few months later (revealing a more accurate picture of who they truly are). I just want you to be mindful this pattern exists if you aren't already. I fell prey to this too many times to count. I often mistook rushed relationships and friendships for extreme chemistry, only to be fooled later. Lao Tzu, the ancient Chinese philosopher and writer, said, "The flame that burns twice as bright burns half as long." A slow-developing friendship or relationship is typically a healthy and long-lasting one.

Identifying Codependent Traits

This section won't apply to all of you, but it may apply to some. For those it does resonate with, this information can be helpful and worth looking into deeper in a therapy setting. Once I discovered what codependency actually was, I noticed it was the root of my relationship issues. It gave me clarity on what areas I needed to work on specifically. For example, finding healthy friendships and partners makes a lot of sense on paper, but when it comes to executing, you may feel bored by the sound of a healthy and mature connection. Chaotic and stressful relationships may be all you've ever known; therefore those dynamics are most familiar to you. It's a fact that we tend to migrate toward familiarity, despite logic. This is common among people who display codependent traits. If you find yourself more comfortable caring for others than for yourself, more comfortable being heavily enmeshed in helping solve other's issues, or if you find yourself attracting "wounded" partners or friends, this may apply to you. There are several different ways codependency can manifest from a young age, and then that becomes your programming for future relationships. You repeat the familiar patterns ingrained in your psyche and wonder why you keep getting disappointed time and time again. Recovering from codependency will require you to dig a little deeper into the wounds of your past. It will require you to lovingly heal those parts of yourself that you haven't believed are worthy of your own love and attention. If this resonates with you at all, like I mentioned earlier, I encourage you to spend some time researching this topic a little more in depth (such as what causes codependency and how to recover from these patterns). There are plenty of good books, podcasts, and Instagram accounts addressing this issue that can be comforting and make you feel less alone. As I mentioned, this would be an important topic to dive into with the help of a therapist.

If you identify with the above descriptions, there is absolutely nothing wrong with you, nothing at all. When my therapist (at the time) told me she thought I displayed codependent traits, I was offended, ashamed, and perplexed. When I did some more research, so many things made sense. I realized this is not something to be ashamed of. In fact, I found many of the traits are tied to loving people so fiercely, giving people too many chances, and wanting to help, yet not giving yourself that same amount of (much deserved) love, respect, and attention. All of these things expose you to being extra vulnerable to people who have a tendency to manipulate and exploit you for their own personal gain. Then, when you really need them (and you assume they will return the favor), they are nowhere to be found. Not to mention, in these types of scenarios, you most often forgive them without an apology because you want to see the good in people. In order to break codependent habits, you will need to be brave and patient enough to educate yourself and make new decisions until identifying what's healthy in a relationship feels more like second nature. This will require work, and it may at times feel hard to accept this label at first, but I promise you it will be worth it. Finally breaking the cycle of toxic partners and friendships once and for all, while learning to love yourself and respect yourself, is an all-around win. If this resonates with you, I encourage you to brave this unknown territory and take this journey toward recovery. Discovering this about myself was like discovering a key to my healing journey. I finally had the answers for how to break so many harmful patterns in my life.

Mini Exercise

I want you to try giving yourself a little more credit by trusting your instincts more. If a friend or partner doesn't reply to your texts or messages on a regular basis and it hurts your feelings, don't assume it's because they are busy or they didn't mean to. It's important to pay attention to how people make you feel. Would you ignore them on a regular basis? Chances are, you don't ignore your friends because you care about their feelings and the friendship itself. Sure, mistakes happen every now and then, but a pattern is a pattern and cannot be denied. Does your friend or partner seem to jokingly put you down and say unkind things behind a smile? Do they imply it's a joke, but you don't actually find it that funny, and deep down those comments hurt your feelings? Then, if you tell them you don't agree with that statement, you're labeled as sensitive or told you can't take a joke? You're not overreacting. Your friends (or whomever) shouldn't sow seeds of doubt in you. They should be encouraging you. Chances are, you don't make fun of them in a hurtful way. Why? Because you don't ever want to hurt their feelings. This can also apply to family members, spouses, and significant others. Yes, even family should love and respect your feelings; they aren't exempt. It's important to teach those around you how you want to be treated and create some necessary boundaries if they refuse to adapt.

The main takeaway is to pay attention to the seemingly little things. If a friend or partner hurts your feelings on a regular basis (even in subtle ways), these things add up, these things matter, and these things are revealing how much someone cares about you and how much they do or don't respect you. The hurtful, strange things we choose to ignore from the start are quite often the things that ultimately cause the relationship to end later on down the line. Save yourself the time, mess, and pain from the start by listening to your gut and reflecting on how people treat you. If you feel you have a friend who doesn't realize they are hurting your feelings but has a good heart, then by all means, politely mention to them in a kind way, "Hey, I don't think you realize it, but when you say X about me, it hurts my feelings. Can you please not say that anymore?" or "Hey, when you don't respond to my messages on a regular basis, it makes me feel like you don't care. I just wanted to let you know how it makes me feel in case you don't realize the effect it has on me." Here's the catch: the answer you seek is all in how they respond to your concerns. If they meet you with a defensive attitude, blaming you for being sensitive or overreacting (or even just implying it with a judgmental look), you just learned a whole lot about this relationship. This person doesn't care for you and respect you the way you thought they did, no matter how many kind things they occasionally do for you in the mix (which can certainly be confusing to process). You simply cannot afford to ignore the little things, because they can be extremely telling, and when you add them up, you'll see the impact is bigger than you realize. Please pay attention to how the people in your life make you feel, and please have enough self-respect to create a healthy distance from those people who make you doubt yourself on a regular basis. You don't necessarily need to make a huge statement or shout it from the rooftops. You can slowly but surely start to distance yourself from that person and politely mention when something hurts your feelings and stand your ground. No one can tell you they didn't hurt your feelings; that's only for you to decide. Trust yourself. You are wiser than you even know. You have no reason to doubt yourself, even if a few convincing people make you feel like you should. Chances are, those people are benefiting from your lack of self-respect and boundaries. Choose yourself from now on. I promise you it's not selfish. It shows self-respect (and we all deserve that).

Side note: You may take my advice and realize, *Wow, I don't have many people left in my life anymore.* In fact, you may have no one left. Trust me when I say that in time you will find people who will respect and love you the way you deserve. It may take more time than you thought, but as long as you focus on loving yourself, respecting yourself, and filtering out people who can't offer you the same, the right people will come in time (and you will be so grateful you were patient, even though it often felt lonely and painful). Sometimes your loneliness or isolation is actually your opportunity to get to know yourself better and love yourself more so you can begin attracting the right people into your life. You have to trust the process, even when it hurts, and even when it takes longer than you would like it to. Sometimes space isn't such a bad thing when we are on a healing and self-love journey. During this timeframe, we can finally learn how to develop a kind relationship with ourselves.

7

The Real Glow Up Is When . . .

You Take Care of Your Physical Health

Maintaining your physical health is another important aspect of self-care. When we properly fuel our bodies and keep them strong, we are better equipped to show up for ourselves in all aspects of our lives. In doing so, we will have higher energy levels to get through the day. And in my experience, more confidence as well. It's important that I emphasize my approach to this topic. For starters, I am not a nutritionist. I will be covering this topic from a broader lens, sharing my own experience and what has worked well for me. Secondly, I'm hyperaware of the role diet culture plays in this conversation, as well as the impossible beauty standards set on us to look a certain way and how damaging both of those things can be to our relationship with food, exercise, and overall mental health. Lastly, I know we all have different health goals, or perhaps health conditions, so this is clearly not a one-size-fits-all topic of discussion.

To this day, I still wrestle at times to find peace with my body, which is understandable given the pressure put on us by society to fit a certain aesthetic. This issue started when I was fairly young. I chose (of my own free will) as a third grader to go on my very first diet, which now, looking back, breaks my heart. I remember catching glimpses of MTV as a kid and seeing all the young women in their bikinis during the spring break television specials, thinking, *Wow, they're adults, so why are they skinnier than me? Something must be wrong with me.* That mentality stuck with me for several years when, in fact, I was a healthy child with a little bit of what some people refer to as baby fat. Throughout my life, I've tried almost every diet out there. A couple of the extreme diets got me to my lowest weight, but I was unhappy and sometimes looked malnourished. Being thin never gave me the satisfaction or confidence I thought it would. (Not to mention, I always gained the weight back, and then some, because the diets were not a practical or long-term lifestyle for me.) On the flip side, I've struggled with weight gain where I just didn't feel healthy or comfortable in my body and constantly experienced that helpless feeling of wanting so desperately to lose it. I was frequently caught up in a cycle of failed diet after diet, coupled with the snowball effect of growing shame. It's such a discouraging cycle to be in, and I know firsthand it can feel disheartening. For the longest time, I had an unhealthy relationship with food, exercise, and body image.

Over the course of the last few years, as I began to prioritize my mental health, I've worked on healing my relationship with food. I've done this through eliminating a restrictive mindset of feeling like *I can't have this,* or *this food is "bad"* because when I followed these rules, it created a sense of shame around food, rather than enjoyment. Sure, nutrition is important. We are meant to eat to fuel our bodies, after all. But that doesn't mean we can't enjoy food or find a healthy balance that works for us. I love food, and the less afraid I've become to say this, the less impulsive I feel around it. This has allowed me to listen to my body more and assess its current needs by releasing a fear mindset around what I eat. It has allowed me to think more clearly about my choices without all the anxious mental chatter that diet culture has imposed on my mind over the years. It has helped me simplify things and release unnecessary stress. In terms of exercise, I used to exclusively use it as a tool to alter my physique. I now do my best to focus on how moving my body makes me *feel*. It feels good for my mental health, and it helps me to be more present in my body. Being more present in my body results in more overall confidence. I am now able to exercise from a place of self-love, rather than shame (or punishment).

Personalization Is Key

We all have different food preferences and lifestyle requirements, so personalization is key. You can eat nutrient dense foods that you actually enjoy and that satisfy your hunger, and you can find workouts that are a good fit for you. If you don't already know what these preferences are, it may require some trial and error. It's all about finding the things you like within the health and fitness realm and incorporating them until they feel like a natural, built-in part of your life. In this scenario, treats and candy won't necessarily be your main source of nutrition, but they can still be fun nonetheless. I never feel deprived with this mindset. And guess what? Some weeks aren't so balanced, and I let it happen without harboring any guilt. By maintaining a self-compassionate and flexible mindset around food in these instances, I then look forward to reverting back to balanced meals when I'm ready, and I appreciate how much better I feel when I am adequately fueling my body. This method is a touch-and-go balance. It's so much less stressful than a diet; it's a lifestyle where I don't feel the need to steep in shame (like I did for the majority of my life). Fueling my body is a form of self-care, and I try to remind myself of that when it feels like a chore. I *get* to choose meals that make me feel good, and I *get* to show myself grace when my nutritional balance is lacking.

Disclaimer: If you are tight on finances, it's important to do the best you can with the resources you have, and perhaps that means buying frozen vegetables, generic brands, or canned goods. Please know that you can improvise your meals and tailor them to your budget and still achieve an overall healthy diet. Don't be fooled or discouraged by absolutes or the all-or-nothing mentality. Simply do the best you can with what you have available to you. A little creativity can go a long way.

Taking care of your physical health is a practice, and it's okay if it takes you some time to find your rhythm and balance, or if you find it and then lose it for a bit. Please be gentle on yourself when navigating through all of this because your mental health is equally as important. Rest when your body calls for it, because different periods of life will heed different exercise capabilities. There is no one-size-fits-all approach to physical health and wellness, so I encourage you to find what works best for you in each season of life. It's important to adapt to your current needs without a looming sense of guilt. Have grace with yourself. Remember, you're a human, life can get messy, and all we can do is our best at any given moment. Sometimes your best now isn't going to look the same as your best the weeks or months prior, and that is perfectly okay. However, if your mental resistance is simply about comfort zones and being scared to advocate for a healthier lifestyle, I encourage you to start small. Build up your confidence with bold baby steps, and pay attention to how awesome you feel when you prioritize your health and wellness.

Mindset Matters

No matter what, please remember you are worthy of self-love, and your weight will never define your worth. You are so much more than a number on the scale or a certain pant size, I promise you that. Please be kind to yourself and patient on your health and wellness journey. If it helps you, follow some people in the "body positivity" or "body acceptance" realm online. I follow a few social media accounts that have helped me reevaluate how I see health and wellness through a much more loving and accepting lens. (I'm so grateful we live in a time where this exists.) And as always, if someone's online content makes you feel bad about yourself, whether it be models, actors or actresses, influencers, or people you know personally, feel free to unfollow or mute them if they frequently stir up feelings of unworthiness or shame in you (even if you have respect for them, it doesn't have to be personal). This has been so crucial on my journey of self-love and body acceptance. On social media, I used to follow every model I could because I thought if I looked at these images, it would motivate me into working out or putting down unhealthy foods more often. In reality, though, it just stirred up a bunch of shame, comparison, and recurring feelings of not being good enough. I now know my mindset around body image and diet was not healthy at that time. On the flip side, if you see these types of accounts as inspirational, and they don't incite feelings of shame, by all means, follow their journeys. The beauty is, we all have the choice to decide what content we consume. Only you can determine what feels healthy for your mindset, so please advocate for what makes you feel best.

Release All Judgment

Another thing I find important to suggest is to not be so quick to judge someone else's health journey or body size. There are so many factors that contribute to someone's body type (big or small), and nothing is ever as simple as it seems. Not to mention, it's not your business anyway. You don't know if someone has a medical condition, has experienced or is experiencing severe trauma, struggles with an eating disorder, or is going through a difficult phase of life. I challenge you to remain open-minded about how you see people: see them as the person they are, and focus less on their physical aesthetic. Society has conditioned us to hold a very narrow-minded view on what's healthy, and I encourage you to challenge this conditioning, especially if you find yourself judging someone else. Let's be quicker to love and accept and less likely to jump to conclusions. Let's pay attention to how diet culture and society have conditioned us to think about weight and body image and rewrite the narrative. Let's be kinder to ourselves and kinder to each other. Let's not jump to conclusions about anybody else's health journey. And lastly, let's view health and wellness as an act of self-care and not a determining factor of our self-worth.

Mini Exercise

Take a few minutes to reflect on your relationship with food and exercise. Does it feel good? Is it something you feel shame around? Is there something you can do to minimize or end this shame cycle and to replace it with self-compassion? Are there any nutrition or exercise goals you can personalize and begin to implement in your life? I encourage you to reflect on all of these questions. If you feel that you may be lacking in balanced meals that fuel you or you are lacking in physical movement, perhaps take some time to jot down ideas that suit your preferences. I've found that by taking the time to merely reflect on these things, I am much more likely to incorporate new habits into my routine. Or perhaps you know what you like already, but you're still experiencing some resistance around incorporating some of these new lifestyle habits. In this case, I'd suggest taking bold "baby steps." Have you resisted walking around your neighborhood because it feels intimidating and out of your comfort zone? Start small. Plug in your headphones, fill up your water bottle, and commit to a short walk. I guarantee that when you do it once or twice, that fear will begin to dissipate. Perhaps the next time you make your grocery list, you intentionally take time to jot down some new and healthy recipe ideas. Trial and error will give you the best results and lead you to new habits. Small, actionable steps are often very beneficial in the long term; but in order to get there, you must have the courage to take these bold baby steps. (I'll touch more on this phrase in the next chapter because it's helped me a lot on my journey.) If you're still feeling some resistance around making small, healthy changes, I encourage you to journal about what is holding you back. Explore the fears you have around food and exercise. It's okay if there are heavy emotions tied to your relationship with food; it could be a coping mechanism that helped you survive some extremely challenging times, whether that be restricting or consuming in excess. This is not the time for beating yourself up; this is a time of tender curiosity and reflection. Trust me, if you struggle with this topic, shame is the last thing you need; instead, you need radical self-acceptance, self-compassion, and patience with yourself along the way.

8

The Real Glow Up Is When . . .

You Learn to Dance with Your Fears

I think it's safe to say that many of us feel the effects of fear throughout our lives. Whether it's fear of what other people think, fear of whether we are doing enough, fear of whether we are on the right path, fear of what will come next, or fear of what will happen if we try something new, it's common to be fearful in various ways. However, fear is natural and isn't always a sign that something bad is going to happen or that we need to resist moving forward. In fact, many influential people throughout history have also felt those same restricting feelings, and they didn't allow those fears to hold them back from living their lives. Susan Jeffers, psychologist and popular self-help author, said it best: "Feel the fear, and do it anyway." How I perceive this powerful quote is that if fear is inevitable, we might as well make friends with it while also learning to work through any resistance that comes up for us. It's massively important that we change our relationship with fear if we want to reach our fullest potential in life.

For some of us, fear may be linked to anxiety. It may be deep-rooted and part of our inner programming. Growing up with the belief system that says, "I am not safe," or "I must always be on high alert" is stressful. You may not even trust your inner-guidance system (aka intuition) as a result. This can stir up a good deal of indecision and perpetuate even more fear, resulting in not knowing what an actual threat is versus what just feels like a threat. This whole process can certainly feel like intimidating territory. If this is something you identify with, I would suggest taking some time to get familiar with the part of you that feels this way. Quite often, this part of yourself can be referred to as the "inner child," as I mentioned earlier. The little child within you who grew up on high alert, never feeling they could truly trust themself or the world around them. This is nothing to be ashamed of. In fact, the last thing you need is more shame. This requires gentle self-compassion and a desire to work through these false beliefs. Over time, you will prove to yourself that you are, in fact, safe. That you can trust yourself. That you hold so much insight inside of you without needing to have all the answers ahead of time. I say this because I once lived this way: untrusting, scared, and on high-alert. In fact, this mode hasn't completely gone away, but I actively work on it. I used to feel so overwhelmed by determining what was a healthy sense of fear and what was, instead, my inner programming of never feeling safe. This manifested as an intense need to analyze every little detail and assess all risks at all times (which is quite exhausting).

Journaling has the potential to be your best ally in this process of making friends with your fear and learning to decipher whether there is a threat, or just a perceived threat. When I feel overcome with fears, I like to jot them down and name them (whether it's in my physical journal, or in my readily available notes app on my phone). I like to list all of the fears I am experiencing in that moment. After I get them out, I examine each fear from an objective standpoint, then counter it with an encouraging thought. Many of us tend to gravitate toward thinking of the worst-case scenarios. We forget that there are also best-case scenarios, in contrast, and since we have no way of predicting the future, it's good to entertain both theories of outcome. Additionally, there is power in determining that even in the worst cases, oftentimes we will be okay, we are strong enough to handle it, and we are still safe to proceed.

This brings me to my next tip in "making friends with your fears." Alyssa Mandel, editorial journalist and creative strategist, speaks to this so beautifully. She references the skill I lightly touched on above of "naming your fears" in order to work through them so as not to let them hinder your goals. This quote of hers resonated with me: "Understanding that fear is at play and contributing to procrastination is the first step to overcoming those blocks. Addressing the fear is the next step. Fear doesn't like to be named, but once you call it out you can address it directly." She then talks about naming your fears and offering them compassion: "Don't be shy about naming your fears. Nothing you fear is stupid. You need to have compassion for your fears and the process of overcoming them. When the fear is still unconscious, you can't really realize how it's manifesting in everyday life. You can't address the shame associated with it; it stays hidden and keeps holding you back from growth."

You see, fear is common. Fear is something we all experience in life, and if we let it run the show, it will rob us from living a full one. Those who achieve their dreams are those who make friends with their fears. They get to know them, they create a safe space within themselves to look at their fears up close with a compassionate lens. They understand that their fears are very well-intentioned, with the goal of protecting them. The thing is, even the people you look up to are fearful. They, too, face this same intimidating process at every stage in their career. If you aren't feeling a little fear, then you may be stuck in your comfort zone, and it may be time to shake things up and try something new. This is the beauty of living your life to the fullest and constantly growing and evolving throughout your life. Fear is inevitable; how we choose to work with it (or dance with it) is optional.

Bold Baby Steps

Pursuing several goals over a long period of time can often cause a major sense of overwhelm. I certainly can relate to this—sometimes so much that it seems much easier to not follow through or to quit before even starting. I'd like to share something that's helped me break down this type of fear. One day, I came up with a phrase that was astoundingly comforting and helpful on my journey. It helped me to stay present in my day-to-day life rather than stress about the future tasks or the larger picture at hand. I dedicated myself to implementing something I called "bold baby steps." I previously touched on this phrase in the last chapter, but I would love to dive in and share a bit more behind why I find this phrase so comforting. Let's face it. There are many moving pieces when trying to achieve various goals, let alone several goals at once. This is problematic because anything worth working for requires time and slow and steady growth. Sometimes I can become so stressed and bogged down just thinking about all I will need to accomplish in order to follow through with a goal. It takes me out of the present moment and fills my head with anxious thoughts. I knew I needed to find a way to cut through this overwhelm so I could take important actionable steps in my day-to-day routine. Even the smallest steps felt terrifying, which only filled me with more shame. I knew I had to reframe how I viewed this fear and this resistance. I needed to change the narrative from shame to courage. I did this by recognizing that even the smallest step toward a goal is brave, no matter how silly it may seem. Sometimes the tiny act of taking one actionable step is the bravest thing you could ever do; oftentimes, these small steps create the momentum you need to accomplish your goals. These baby steps can be confidence-building and empowering.

So how did I change this narrative from feeling pathetic and shameful to feeling empowered? I created a phrase for these seemingly small steps that add up to one larger, bigger-picture goal, and I called them *bold baby steps*. The simple act of reframing something as small as working out for twelve minutes when I hadn't worked out in months, or attending my first therapy session when I was terrified to open up to a stranger, or brainstorming the outline of this book when I had no clue how I was ever going to find the strength within me to actually write it. Seemingly small tasks, when aligned with your goals, are brave, and you shouldn't feel shame if they scare you. You deserve to be kind to yourself along the way and to give yourself the credit you've earned. Each step may seem small, but every move forward you make is bold and courageous in its own respect.

Mini Exercise

Do you have some big dreams or goals that you've neglected or avoided due to fear? Chances are, you probably do. (That's perfectly normal; I'm right there with you.) I encourage you to write down a handful of your dreams. They may feel big and scary, or completely out of your realm of possibility. Still, write them down one by one, without holding back. Then, I encourage you to reflect on each goal or dream, and name your fears surrounding that specific pursuit. Reflect on the questions: "What am I scared will happen?" and "Why don't I feel qualified to do this?" Now I invite you, with self-compassion and a fresh perspective, to look at each reason you wrote down and respond with an optimistic attitude of what could go *right*, then provide some reasons why you actually are qualified to accomplish this dream. The goal is to see where your fears are holding you back so you can make space for welcoming in your endless potential. This exercise allows you to see the worst-case scenario and realize that (most of the time) you have nothing to fear. If the worst did occur, you would, in fact, be fine, because humans have a way of being resilient in tough times. Remember, too, that these are simply fears, not truths, and there is so much beautiful potential in stepping out of your comfort zone and choosing to believe in yourself.

9

The Real Glow Up Is When . . .

You Live Out Your Purpose

Friendly reminder: life is short. This chapter isn't about achieving what your family may expect from you, and it isn't about fulfilling society's idea of success and achievement. The message in this chapter is so much deeper. This is about living out your purpose and not only sharing your unique gifts and talents with the world, but also living a life that feels authentic to who you are (in turn, bringing more happiness and ease into your life). Plus, you don't know how many people you could be helping by simply being brave enough to shine your light and to step into your individual calling.

Here's the secret, one that took me a long time to accept and understand: you do not need to have it all figured out right now. In fact, if you do, you are a part of the rare few. Throw out the idea that "by this age" I need to have my whole life figured out. Many of us have our self-esteem tied to this belief: "I must have everything figured out before the end of my twenties (or my thirties, forties, fifties, etc.)." We are deceiving ourselves if we shackle our belief systems to this unattainable standard. For most people, finding your dream career path or life purpose is a bit of a scavenger hunt; it takes trial and error, which then leads to a beautiful accumulation of new skills and more insight into what it is you feel most passionate about. This might not even apply to a career for you. It may look like parenthood, a charitable pursuit, and/or a dream hobby that fulfills you. And to clarify, this is not to say you have to pick this or that. Many people find purpose in multiple aspects of their lives. However, while sharing a bit of my own story, I'll be applying this concept in terms of career path.

While trying to find my purpose, and a job that felt best aligned with who I am and what I want to make my life's work about, I felt very discouraged along the way. However, hindsight is twenty-twenty, and often incredibly revealing. I've since discovered the value of this seemingly random career path I experienced. I think many other people can relate to this frustration of not knowing what path is best suited for them long term. I used to be so hard on myself for not having it all figured out. I was desperate to know what the elusive *it* was, and I wanted to know when I'd find *it*.

I pursued and worked in five completely different career fields before I found my sweet spot (six if you count the current one, which is writing and creating content around self-love, self-care, and healing). I had attended a technical college for a couple of years in hopes to become a nurse, then realized in CNA clinicals that it was not at all the right field for me. I then pursued and went to school for broadcast journalism, interned at my local news station, created a demo reel, graduated, was offered a reporting job in a nearby small town, hitting all my goal points, and then realized that this job was not the right one for me either. I followed that career by entering into corporate sales and marketing, and (surprise, surprise) again found it was not something I wanted to continue on with. Next, I worked in an executive administrative role for a global technology company. I had a feeling this job wasn't going to be a long-term situation either, but it paid the bills and was a safe landing space while I figured things out for a couple of years. My next venture was the path of entrepreneurship where I launched my online clothing boutique. This was exciting and new; however, I lacked the long-term passion for retail. I felt there had to be something better suited for me. This was an amazingly difficult decision, so I even tried to come up with ways to make this business feel more meaningful. It was my "baby," so to speak, and it felt weird to even consider abandoning that dream. I had planned to switch over to ethically sourced pieces. I thought this change might spark more passion in me for the retail clothing career path. I had followed through with the research component of this, but I just had a strange inner pull to instead pause and take time to actually reflect on this decision more before I financially committed to the big rebrand. I'm relieved I did this because with the time I took to step away for a while and truly think about it, I realized my passion isn't in retail, not even with the ethical changes I had dreamed up. Entrepreneurship, however, would continue to be a part of my story.

If I didn't continuously honor that little voice inside me that said, "This isn't it" each time I had realized a certain career wasn't for me, I wouldn't have landed at this place where I'm at now. A place where I feel so aligned with my purpose, so fulfilled and so passionate (everything I was seeking). As mentioned, I feel my purpose is correlated with writing and creating, as well as sharing my story to help guide others on their journey. I had no idea at the time, but this has been my life's work to date. I've been committed to the goal of healing, growing, evolving, and finding meaning in my life's journey throughout all five of the previous career fields I had tried out. I've often had this feeling that life is too short to waste time living lukewarm. I've strived to be the best version of myself that I can possibly be (to a fault at times because this can breed harmful issues like perfectionism). It has been increasingly important to me that I don't take my life for granted, that I embrace life fully and continue to learn from all of my experiences. This is the root of my work now.

It's funny because I've heard people say things along the lines of, "In hindsight, your life's purpose will make sense to you. You will understand why you had to work in various fields and positions. The skills you've acquired will not be put to waste; they will serve a purpose some way in your future plans." I've since realized how true this all is. I learned there is no shame in trying out new career paths and allowing life to guide you. It's because of where I've been that I now feel confident to take this new direction. None of it was a waste at all. And the fear that it "took me too long" or "wasted my precious time" or made me seem all over the place, like I just couldn't commit to something, was only my inner bully and critic at play. I think people should be proud of themselves for trying out new things and not remaining stagnant for the sake of comfort or the approval of society. I finally had a full-circle moment when this realization fully impacted me. I developed patience, faith, a diverse skill set, built a vast network of connections, learned to trust my intuition, and it all led me to exactly where I needed to be at the right time.

The reason I felt it important to share this with you is because I know many can relate to those intense feelings of frustration and fear that are fueled by not knowing what purpose you are most aligned with. I believe this is a common modern-day struggle. However, I think there is a certain trust that can take place to help dissolve some of this frustration on your way to figuring it out. In the waiting, there can be so much wisdom gained and character development taking place. In hindsight, you would not want to rob yourself of the process. I believe if you can continue to try new things, trust your intuition, avoid settling, and release the fear of what others will think, you will ultimately end up where you are meant to be. It will all make sense in perfect time. We just need to trust the bigger picture and remove harsh timelines and expectations.

I have learned some helpful tips along the way that I believe could make your career journey slightly easier and smoother, and I'd love to share them with you. I would like to also include the disclaimer that I know hard work, dedication, flexibility, and taking bold, calculated chances are important and have allowed me the opportunities I've shared with you above. However, it would be completely ignorant for me to not acknowledge my privilege in these scenarios (White privilege, socioeconomic privilege, the privilege of good health, the privilege of being a cisgender, straight female—not to mention the privilege of working in industries that aren't overly male dominated). By no means do I want this to be a discouraging disclaimer, but I do find it massively important that I don't accidently oversimplify or trivialize other people's career obstacles.

Now I'd like to share what's helped me on my career journey.

Job Shadowing / Informational Interviews

A common occurrence in my story is that I job shadowed through various internships to catch a real-life glimpse of the "behind the scenes" of desired careers. Through this process, I was usually able to learn enough to decipher whether they were a good fit for me or not. Now here's the cool part: not everyone needs to intern or work in a specific job role to obtain this type of information. More often than not, I've learned that many different fields will allow you to job shadow for the day, or for a few days. Doing this allows you to see what the job entails firsthand, and you can ask questions about what the job and lifestyle is like from someone who is actually living it. Another option to gain further insight would be to schedule an informational interview. This could be a coffee date, a phone call, an online video meeting, etc. Most of the time, people will be brutally honest with you because they want you to be aware of certain things up front. You can glean a ton of information from simply emailing an optimal point person at a company (found through a little research or asking around), kindly expressing interest in the role (doesn't hurt to flatter them a bit), and request if they'd let you job shadow or schedule an informational interview at their convenience and by their preferred method. You may have to kindly follow up if you don't hear back and perhaps request them to put you in touch with the correct person for that specific role. It takes some effort and being a little bit bold, but if you don't ask, you will never receive. Not to mention, you could save yourself valuable time in the long run by simply stepping out of your comfort zone for a few short moments. Trust me, job shadowing is much easier than blindly pursuing a career path only to realize (after investing time and money) it's a terrible fit for you. Also, many people are surprisingly open and receptive to these types of requests. You may even find a mentor in all of this. If you get an opportunity to job shadow or schedule an informational interview, by all means, please be flexible and work with their schedule, and always be punctual and respectful. This person is taking precious time out of their day to help you gain insight, and it's very generous of them to accommodate you. Many of them have had mentors in the past, and this is their way of paying it forward, but it doesn't mean it's convenient or easy for them to carve out time. Please show your appreciation by writing a thank-you note. If it feels appropriate, buy them a thoughtful gift, like a fun coffee mug, or better yet, find out their drink of choice and bring them their preferred coffee or tea when you see them each time. A little bit of appreciation can go a long way.

Forget What Other People Think

I think Eleanor Roosevelt said it best: "Do what you feel in your heart to be right, for you'll be criticized anyway." It's so easy to fall into the trap of basing our decisions off of what other people will approve of.

There is no doubt in my mind that we are social creatures by nature. The problem is, you shouldn't have to compromise what you love to make others feel comfortable. This will, without a doubt, backfire and limit the amount of joy and fulfillment you will achieve in life. Not to mention, even when you play it safe, there are people who will judge, mock, or call it boring. If judgement is unavoidable, then why not follow your heart?

I'm not saying it's easy to let go of the fear of what other people will think of you. In fact, some scientists believe it's hardwired in our human instincts to strive for a sense of belonging and safety, which then leads to the constant seeking of approval from others. The thought behind this being that at one point in humanity, fighting to achieve this sense of belonging was considered essential to our survival. Here's the thing though: fear doesn't necessarily serve you the same way anymore, and you have to work at unlearning that survival technique in order to achieve your dreams and follow your life's true purpose. You are safe to step out of that confined little box you've been hiding in your whole life. You are safe to try something new or unconventional. People need you to step into your truth because your unique gifts and abilities aren't meant to lie dormant forever. They exist for a reason.

I have to say, writing this book feels unbelievably unsafe to me. In fact, I haven't even told many people I'm writing this because of how scary it can feel to admit it. I fear people will laugh at me, judge me, and even view me as egotistical or completely out of my realm. Those are the initial and recurring fears that arise in me when I'm feeling scared about following my dreams. The thing is, that's my inner bully and critic attempting to scare me into playing it safe, but it's not in my best interest. If this book could help even just a small handful of people, and I can say I followed through with something I felt called to do with every fiber of my being, then I don't care if someone calls me egotistical or out of my league. Life is too damn short to worry about who will judge you. Like I mentioned before, the judgment from others is inevitable (and rarely has anything to do with you). It may terrify you at first, but I hope you embrace the narrative that you are worthy of following your dreams.

Your unique gifts deserve to be seen and not sheltered from the world. You are safe to embrace your life, especially if the only thing holding you back is this fear that people won't accept you. Can I let you in on a secret? "Your people," the people meant to be in your life, will accept you no matter what (as long as you aren't harming yourself or anyone else). Step into your truth unapologetically, and remember, as long as you approve of yourself, you already have all you need. Denying your dreams is denying yourself the joy that comes with following your truth. Trust me when I say, those "callings," feeling pulled toward certain endeavors, aren't by accident; they are tailor-made for you. You just need to work through those fears one step at a time and persevere despite how scary it can feel. Replace your fearful thoughts with encouraging ones, and keep moving forward. I believe in you, and I fully support your decision to follow those dreams. It's okay if not everyone cheers you on. Not everyone has to understand; ultimately, it's *for you* to understand.

Don't Be Ashamed of Being a Beginner

It's ridiculously easy to fall into the trap of feeling "not good enough" or "not experienced enough" while developing a new skill set. In fact, I'd say the default mindset most of us feel when trying something new is, *Who do I think I am?* The truth is, you may not know what you're doing, but the only way to learn is to allow yourself to be vulnerable enough to embrace being a beginner. There should be no shame in trying something new. Most people are so insecure about feeling inadequate that they withhold permission from themselves to even start something new. I'm right there with you. Sometimes I feel paralyzed with fear when starting a new endeavor. I have to work at accepting the humility that comes with being a beginner. Every single person, no matter their craft, started off as a student, a newcomer. They were just brave enough to take those steps forward and set their ego aside to learn something new and keep at it day by day. This process takes patience and grace with oneself.

Additionally, we can choose to see mistakes as learning opportunities and inexperience as a blank canvas to work with. Oftentimes, we are so hard on ourselves that we don't allow ourselves to start something new. Know that this fear is very real, but you get to choose whether you let it hold you back from following your dreams or not. With a little time and experience, everything will start to feel easier and more natural, I guarantee it. Please, be patient with yourself along the way.

Note: The people who judge you for trying something new are usually revealing their own insecurities. These types of people are typically not brave enough or bold enough to take a chance and blaze new territory. So in order to feel "right" in their way of being and in their way of "playing it safe," they question and attack your courage. Please don't take it personally. It has absolutely nothing to do with you and everything to do with their own decisions and insecurities.

The "Third Door" Theory

Alex Banayan is the author of the bestselling book *The Third Door*. In this book he describes the often unique and overlooked tactics when pursuing lofty goals. Banyan has impressively interviewed some of the world's wealthiest and most influential people in the world with none other than the determination and creativity described in his book.

In it, he explains the Third Door theory:

> "Life, business, success . . . it's just like a nightclub.
> There are always three ways in. There's the First Door:
> the main entrance, where 99 percent of people wait in
> line, hoping to get in. The Second Door: the VIP
> entrance, where the billionaires and celebrities slip
> through. But what no one tells you is that there is
> always, always . . . the Third Door. It's the entrance
> where you have to jump out of line, run down the
> alley, bang on the door a hundred times, crack open
> the window, sneak through the kitchen—there's
> always a way."

My biggest takeaway from his teachings would be to embrace creativity when approaching your goals (think outside the box), and don't let apparent setbacks discourage you from pursuing your dreams. For example, if you're having trouble getting in contact with someone at a certain company you want to work for, ask yourself if you know someone who works there who you could reach out to? Acquaintance or not, politely reach out to that person and see if they could put you in touch with the hiring manager, or see if they'd meet you for an informational interview so you could ask how to get your "foot in the door." Need another example? Let's say you wrote a book, then self-published it, but you don't know how to market it and create a buzz to increase your sales. What if you were to research celebrities, authors, or influencers you admire who seem like they'd be interested in your material, and you wrote them a thoughtful card and mailed them a free copy of your book. If you did this with one hundred books, then maybe, just maybe, one of those influential people may feel compelled to read it. Perhaps they loved the book so much that they reached back out to you, promoted your book on their social media accounts, and put you in touch with a connection who could further your writing career. What's the point here? Don't be afraid to get creative and take calculated risks. Many people play it safe and stick to the status quo when pursuing their dreams. Dare to think outside the box if you are presented with challenges or roadblocks along the way; believe in the magic of a creative approach. Don't let a "road less traveled" technique scare you out of something that could actually set you apart on your journey to achieving your dreams.

Disclaimer: Even if you live a purposeful life, don't be surprised when it still feels like hard work. The key difference is, it won't be the kind of work that drains your soul; it will ultimately fulfill you.

Mini Exercise

Take a moment to daydream. Set aside all of your fears and truly take this time to brainstorm. Write down what you're most passionate about—what you would do for free if money wasn't an issue. Maybe this causes you stress or tension because you wish you knew but you don't, and that's okay. Try your hardest to release all expectations right now, and allow yourself to have fun with this exercise. You might only have a vague idea, but keep at it. The goal here is to simply create space to imagine different possibilities.

Here are some examples:

- I love caring for animals.

- I love mentoring my friends and motivating people.

- I love designing beautiful spaces in my home.

- I love financial planning and organizing.

- I love cooking and baking.

- I love creating fun content.

- I love designing workout and nutrition plans.

- I love to make art.

- I love to assist with a good cause.

There is no wrong answer here. In this brainstorming scenario, there is no pressure to make society or your friends and family approve of you, and there are no financial limitations over what's practical. The purpose of this exercise is to remove all external pressures for a moment and begin to embrace what lights you up, what feels most natural to you. If your inner critic starts to chime in and make you feel underqualified for certain endeavors, please pay attention to that and replace those thoughts with uplifting ones, such as, *What if **I am** qualified for this, and just never realized it?*

The truth is, there is an abundance of pressure in this world coming from all directions, making it hard to tap into that part of yourself that knows what you like and dislike. Some of us have never let ourselves dream because it felt like there was no room for it in our lives. This exercise is to help you get in touch with your true passions—not what looks good on the outside but what feels good on the inside. What you choose to do with this information is entirely up to you. Maybe you make time to learn more about that interest; maybe you start following people on social media who work in that field; maybe you daydream about it from time to time or start a new hobby; and maybe you are already clear on what you're passionate about, and this practice was just further validation for you. I encourage you to keep an open mind with your goals and be kind to yourself throughout this process. Instead of thinking, *Yeah, right*, try thinking, *Why not?* Allow yourself to dream.

10

The Real Glow Up Is When . . .

You Make Time to Connect with Others

I define connection as the energy that exists between people when they feel seen,
heard and valued, when they can give and receive without judgement, and when
they derive sustenance and strength from the relationship.
—Brené Brown

Connection is a tricky one, but it's an important facet of life. I didn't
realize I struggled with this until recent years. As I got older, my social
anxiety became more prevalent, and I lost touch with how to truly
slow down and connect with people. I conversed, I exchanged
pleasantries, and I put myself "out there," but I knew something was
missing. In my case, feelings of anxiety made it hard for me to be
present in conversations. I was overthinking what I was saying, how I
came across, how to best please people, and how to feel "safe" in my
exchanges by withholding vulnerable information about myself. In
doing so, I was unknowingly missing out on the opportunity for close
connections in my life. I knew this was an area I wanted to improve
upon. Through some research and trial and error, I realized a few key
things that were missing in my conversations with others. The good
news is, it wasn't too much of a challenge to implement these new
habits. It just took a little intentionality. Human connection is vital and

creates a mutual sense of belonging in relationships; which we all deserve. Throughout this chapter, I'll share the key things I learned to help me better connect with people.

Being Present and Slowing Down

Feeling caught up in anxiety can definitely take us out of the present moment. Because of this, I had to remind myself to slow down my pace, to take a deep breath, and to truly listen when others are speaking. We are often trying to figure out how to respond to people, yet we aren't actually listening intently to the content of what they are saying—the emotions, the vulnerability, the fears, the excitement. I urge you to try something new: be fully present and listen to what the other person has to say. Take a pause before responding if you need to digest what someone said. There is only a rush if you create one.

This is also relevant in virtual/digital interactions. So often when receiving a direct message or a text from someone, I have felt the need to respond right away, resulting in a rushed response rather than a grounded one. There is no rule stating you must reply instantly. What does slowing down your response let you do? It lets you react from a genuine place rather than a place of anxiety. It lets you thoughtfully approach situations without thinking, *Wait, that was weird. Why did I just say that?* Rather, you can engage in a new and calm way, allowing space for real connection to take place by not rushing and putting unnecessary pressure on yourself. Slowing down, both in person and online, is imperative if you want to truly connect with others.

Sit with People in Their Struggles

If you're anything like me, you may be an idealist or a fixer. Or perhaps watching others close to you face challenges can feel really uncomfortable. You may have the best intentions and want to help, leading you to rattle off advice when someone shares a hardship. Here's the thing: well-intentioned or not, most people simply want to feel seen, heard, and have their pain validated. They want to feel less alone by vocalizing some of these struggles with you, and that's it. Most of the time they aren't seeking advice unless they specifically ask for it. As much as you may have great advice, it's best to be mindful of how you approach these situations if you are inclined to want to fix things. If someone asks for your opinion, then by all means share away. It's common to feel compelled to share suggestions with the other person almost immediately after they share their struggles with you. We don't always realize this, but sometimes it can make us really uncomfortable to "sit" in someone's pain with them. By *sit*, I mean to allow someone's discomfort to simply be, without wishing it away for them or talking in platitudes. You are a witness to their pain, and you are saying by your actions, "Your struggle is not too much for me. I'll sit with you as you experience this." As counterintuitive as it may seem, by doing this, you help the other person feel less alone, and this is the beauty of why it's so impactful. Your presence says, "I see your pain. I understand your pain. And I am here for you. You're not alone in this, no matter how uncomfortable the situation is. You are safe to feel big emotions, and I will not reject you or minimize them for my own comfort."

You may be wondering *how* to validate someone's pain and sit with them in it, asking yourself, *What does that even look like?* It looks like simply listening and acknowledging what they shared with you by repeating it back to them in your own words. For example, if your friend or partner says, "Work has been such a challenge lately. I can't seem to catch a break. It just feels like there are constant issues to fix." You could say in response, "Wow, it sounds like work has been super overwhelming for you. It seems like that would be very tiring to manage." The goal here is to make them feel seen, heard, and understood. This goes a long way—trust me. Even if it feels silly or incomplete, it's the most helpful way you can respond and offer support.

Feel free to ask questions and engage in conversation, but I encourage you to hold back from diving into advice-giving tendencies. Sometimes just talking things through with someone can help the other person better process what positive changes they could make without you offering any suggestions. Not to mention, this saves you from being that bitter friend who always gives advice but feels frustrated because "no one seems to take it," which tends to make people feel undervalued or, perhaps, not trusted. The thing is, humans are magnificently intuitive; oftentimes, we know what we need to do, but we need to work through our own stuff in our own timeframe. You may give the best and most applicable advice ever, but if that person has something else inside holding them back from taking action, your advice doesn't help them right now; in fact, it may just evoke shame. That's why it is more powerful to sit with them in their pain or struggle, validate their situation, and allow them to process things with you by compassionately listening and asking thoughtful questions. A little bit goes such a long way. At first, it may be challenging to think about your every response, but eventually, these habits will become second nature to you (even if you slip up from time to time). I guarantee if you can practice this, you will feel more connected with people, and vice versa too.

Mini Exercise

If you find that you relate to the issues I described in this chapter of not feeling as connected to people as you'd like, I invite you to practice these techniques. Next time you connect with or check in with a friend, I encourage you to practice the art of slowing down before responding, while also practicing the validation technique mentioned above. It may make you feel really uncomfortable, or it may feel unnatural to sit with others in the "pain" of their current issue (and that's okay), but I encourage you to resist jumping into fix-it mode. Repeat back to them what you're hearing, and validate that it sounds hard, challenging, overwhelming, or confusing. Create space for true connection by learning how to embrace your discomfort in those moments so you can be there for them in a new, supportive way. A thoughtful follow-up question is, *How can I best support you right now?*

Please know you can always come back to this practice, start over, and create new habits (even if it takes some trial and error). No matter what, I know you have good intentions, but this is about allowing yourself to truly connect with people in new and beautiful ways. Connection is such a special aspect of life, and I hope you can give yourself that gift. A gift that serves not just you but the person on the other end as well. Showing up intentionally is a clear display of love and consideration.

11

The Real Glow Up Is When . . .

You Assess Your Drinking Habits

Bear with me, I'm not here to judge, I promise. The thing is, I can't judge because I've had quite an interesting relationship with alcohol myself, and I spent thirteen years trying to get it right. From the ripe young age of fifteen, I began drinking socially. I ran in a circle that you could call "trouble," always looking for a party to escape to. I was most definitely in a rebellious phase of my life and quickly learned that alcohol helped me feel more outgoing and less stressed (in the moment, of course). My relationship with alcohol was complicated, new, and exciting. Throughout those thirteen years, I experienced embarrassing moments of oversharing, nasty falls, mystery bruises, throwing up, picking silly fights with my husband—not to mention, the worst hangovers ever. I thought I had gotten to a slightly "classier" place with drinking in my late twenties because I stopped taking shots at bars or parties and mainly stuck to beer and wine. The issue was, I had grown accustomed to drinking around two or three glasses of wine on almost a nightly basis. It had become an ingrained coping mechanism for me to deal (or not deal) with my anxiety issues. I knew deep down I needed to cut back, or figure something out, but it just felt like my habits were so established that when I tried to cut back, I would think, *Oh well, why not have a glass?*

Eventually, as mentioned before, my dad passed away unexpectedly, and I turned to alcohol to cope with the pain. It became increasingly more evident that my relationship with alcohol was not a healthy one, and although my life was perfectly intact, I felt alcohol had held me back in many ways from truly stepping into the real growth and transformation I wanted for myself. I knew I was capable of more, and I knew I deserved a much healthier lifestyle (both mentally and physically). Shortly after that, my husband and I talked about the possibility of abstaining from alcohol altogether, and we both agreed it would be a really positive change for us, both personally and for our relationship. To have each other's support through this new life change was uniquely special, and it no doubt made the process that much smoother.

What does my experience have to do with anything? Well, the decision of cutting out alcohol has been such a beautiful change for my personal life, mental health, and for evolving and stepping more fully into my authentic self. Does this mean I'm suggesting everyone quit drinking alcohol? No, I know that some of you already have a healthy relationship with drinking and it may not be necessary (unless it's something that intrigues you). However, if you can relate to having a dysfunctional relationship with alcohol, I urge you to explore the *possibility* of quitting. I know this is usually scary territory to explore, so please bear with me. Maybe you begin by *considering* what that might look like for you. Maybe you don't make this decision right now, *but you plant the seed*, and one day, if you have an urge or intuition to quit, you revisit that seed.

The thing about alcohol is that it's often used as a coping mechanism. When I gave up drinking, I was presented with a great deal of unprocessed emotions that had been somewhat strategically avoided the previous thirteen years. It took me a few months of being in a funk and feeling socially awkward without it before I found my footing. For some, this coping mechanism is like medicine; perhaps alcohol numbed and "protected" you from previous unresolved trauma. The question to ask is: To what extent is alcohol helping you manage your pain? This answer could be telling based on how much support you may need in order to quit. Additionally, there are genetic factors that predispose you to addiction. All in all, if you identify drinking alcohol as a coping mechanism, this is not something to be ashamed of. It's a human response to a deep-seated pain within you. If the topic of quitting is something that is piquing your interest, I suggest you look more into the "sober curious" movement. There are more and more people choosing an alcohol-free lifestyle by the day; slowly but surely shattering the stigmas around sobriety. The sober curious community is inspiring and filled with helpful resources and fresh perspectives around the benefits of quitting.

Marketing tactics often portray alcohol as an obvious choice, creating feelings of entitlement: "Why wouldn't you drink?" or "You don't drink? What do you mean?" Often, ads and movies glamorize the act of pouring a drink the second you get home from a long day at work, or enjoying a glass of wine after a long day spent with your children, or perhaps the old rule of "all celebrations call for a bottle of wine or a bottle of champagne." People are constantly spinning this narrative that it's the cure-all, a nonnegotiable, a way of life. Millie Gooch, CEO of the UK-based Sober Girl Society, speaks to this topic often. She does a fantastic job at shedding light on the psychology behind the marketing of alcohol. I won't dive too deep into this topic, but it's a blatant fact that alcohol companies work extraordinarily hard to sell the idea that you should drink. They are constantly working hard to normalize and reinforce an alcohol-based lifestyle. So if you find yourself feeling weird about the thought of not drinking, you are not alone; it has been programmed into our psyche for the majority of our lives. Am I here to bash alcohol marketing campaigns? No. In fact, some of these companies are realizing the increasing demand for non-alcoholic substitutes and are responding accordingly. I think that's great. I also think it's important to highlight that if the idea of quitting feels weird to you, that's completely normal. We've all been taught to think in this status quo mindset: "You're an adult; therefore you drink." Movies, television, and advertising have created the narrative that drinking away your pain after a bad day is normal. If you don't identify with having a semi-problematic relationship with alcohol, then the old saying, "Drink to get happier; don't drink to get happy," may be a good rule of thumb for you regardless. This school of thought could encourage you to process your emotions rather than numbing them and then having these issues resurface later because you never dealt with them.

At the end of the day, I think it's important (from personal experience) to make sure your drinking habits are in line with who you want to be. So if there is any conflict between the two, I suggest taking a closer look at how you might adjust your relationship with alcohol, whether that be changing your habits or quitting altogether, but no one can make that decision for you. You have the power to decide what you want your life to look and feel like. You have full permission to make decisions that bring you happiness and good health. If you are concerned about friendships ending or seeming like the wet blanket of your friend group, you may want to remind yourself that any friend who truly supports you will respect your decision, even if it takes them a moment to adjust. Your value shouldn't be in how much or how frequently you can drink alcohol. You have so much more to offer the world than that. If someone shuns you for this, you did not lose a friend; you lost a drinking buddy.

My Tips and Takeaways from Living the Dry Life

If you are curious about quitting alcohol or cutting back, but you feel overwhelmed by how you would even begin to implement this lifestyle change, I feel you. I felt severely intimidated by the process myself.

Looking back, I found certain things to be majorly helpful along the way, and I'd love to share these tips with any of you who are interested. The first thing I found to be immediately beneficial was to search for an online sober community. I followed a handful of Instagram accounts where others shared their experiences and their lifestyle of not drinking alcohol anymore. I could have chosen to interact with people more, but I mostly observed from afar, and that was enough for me to feel less isolated in my decision. There are many sobriety-focused accounts and podcasts that are fun, vibrant, inspiring, and can help you feel less alone in your endeavors. As mentioned, you can also look into the sober curious movement for many helpful resources.

When it comes to social outings, I found it helpful to always be prepared with alternative drink options in hand (whether this be in my home or at a social function). It's helpful to have your go-tos, because many people hosting an adult event will forget that not everyone drinks, resulting in them neglecting to provide non-alcoholic options. This is why coming prepared with your own drinks is so helpful. Being prepared can also extend to other environments too. I enjoy kombucha or soda water when I'm at home (while cooking a meal, taking a bath, or watching my favorite show). If my friends invite me to a dive bar, I'll sometimes have a Red Bull or a non-alcoholic beer (most bars will have one or two non-alcoholic beer options). If I'm at a nice brunch or happy hour, I like to order a fun mocktail, if it's available. When looking for a healthier option, I opt for soda water and muddled lime.

Another thing that oftentimes feels scary is not knowing how to talk about this decision with others. I've found that less is more. There is no need to explain all the little details for why you chose to quit (unless you enjoy sharing this, then by all means do). You don't owe anyone a big explanation, even though it might feel that way at first. For me, I found this to be intimidating. I didn't want to kill the vibe, make others feel guilty for drinking, or act like I was superior. If someone notices I'm not drinking, I'm honest and say, "I'm not drinking tonight," or "No, thank you." Most people don't press the issue too much. And even though it might feel awkward, most of the time they are accepting of it nonetheless. Some will say, "Come on, how about just one?" or will press the issue in some way to guilt you into joining them. In these instances, I laugh, say no thank you, and walk away. This is all up to you, but at the end of the day, the people who are meant to stay in your life will see your value as much more than just a drinking buddy and will respect your decision to not drink.

The next tip is practicing self-care for those stressful moments. It's helpful to identify ahead of time some self-soothing, calming, and grounding techniques for when you do have truly challenging days. Because let's face it, we all have these moments. Identifying what these techniques are for you is incredibly helpful. For me, that involves Epsom salt baths, hot tea, a good meal, a sweet treat, guided meditations, stretching, a funny show, a hug from my husband, journaling, soothing music, and being honest with myself and simply vocalizing if I had a hard day. You will learn, over time, what tools best enable you to decompress in these moments. They will no doubt be important resources for you to take care of yourself.

The last bit of parting wisdom I'd like to share on this topic is regarding checking off your "firsts"—attending your first sober wedding, sporting event, concert, dive bar, wine tasting invite, birthday, anniversary, vacation or friends trip, Thanksgiving, house party, Christmas, or family event. If you are used to consuming alcohol on any given occasion, the first time doing these things sober can feel jarring, especially if you've relied on alcohol to boost your social skills or reduce your stress at events. Please know it is completely normal to feel like a fish out of water when experiencing these firsts. I can genuinely say once I checked each of them off my list, they were far less intimidating the second time around. So if this is you, please be kind to yourself in these moments and (as mentioned before) always come prepared with beverages to be sure there are options for you. Also, feel free to celebrate these firsts! These firsts can feel unquestionably challenging and nerve-wracking, and checking them off your list is a big deal. Please do not feel shameful or guilty if these are hard experiences for you. Truthfully, you may even find it difficult to enjoy the experience if you are riddled with anxiety and discomfort. This is all the more reason to be kind to yourself and celebrate your accomplishment. I don't share this to scare you; I share this to let you know it's completely normal to feel tense or drained from these firsts. Just remind yourself: these events will get so much easier the second time around; it won't always feel so challenging.

Mini Exercise

If this chapter sparked some discomfort in you, or perhaps inspired you to think differently about your relationship with alcohol, I encourage you to reflect a little more on this. Like I said earlier, maybe you don't feel ready to make any decisions right now. Maybe you simply plant the seed of curiosity and begin to consider the possibility of a lifestyle change involving alcohol. Consider journaling about the type of life you envision for yourself, and reflect on whether you can picture your current drinking habits meshing well with that vision. If not, maybe see what you *do* envision that relationship with alcohol to look like. It's possible that means no alcohol at all if you've learned you can't trust yourself to set those ideal boundaries. No matter what, please be gentle on yourself while you explore these possibilities. You have nothing to be ashamed of; you are a human doing your very best to cope with life. I have no judgement toward anyone when it comes to this topic; however, I do have a massive amount of empathy because I know how hard it is to navigate these issues. Oftentimes, we already know the answer to these questions deep down, and we can tap into that if we are simply able to create the necessary space to listen to that little (yet meaningful) voice within.

12

The Real Glow Up Is When . . .

You Give Yourself Permission

Throughout the first twenty-eight years of my life, there were many things that I knew would be good for me, but I just didn't make them a priority. It's hard to explain, but it was almost like a subconscious choice I had made, as if for some reason I felt other people deserved certain things but I, somehow, did not. It was a form of self-sabotage, really. An invisible weight I let hold me down in life. I held myself back from developing good habits, practicing self-care, pursuing certain goals, and standing confidently in my power. There are many things in my life that I denied myself the pleasure of simply because I didn't give myself permission to do them. I felt I was waiting for someone else to say, "Hey! You deserve to feel good and take care of yourself. Allow yourself to do _____ more often." Essentially, I was expecting someone else to hand me my power, as if it didn't exist otherwise. When I finally realized that I was giving away my power and indirectly self-sabotaging myself in these small ways (which definitely add up in the larger picture), I knew this was something I had to work on. I have goosebumps just writing this now because I know how life-changing this realization has been for me in such a short amount of time, and I want that for you too. We need to give ourselves permission to live out our very best life, and we need to take care of ourselves in ways that reinforce this narrative.

This topic may overwhelm you a bit, and perhaps it conjures up feelings of shame. Please, by all means, disinvite those thoughts from this discussion. In no way is this a chapter on "you need to do more." We have enough of that voice pulsing through our heads on a daily basis. This is a chapter about allowing yourself permission to implement the habits that result in you feeling your best. It's also about finding a healthy balance in your life so you can take care of yourself adequately, because you deserve that level of care and consideration. Maybe I'm the one who initially needs to give you permission. Right now, I am telling you from the bottom of my heart that you deserve to take care of yourself just as much as anyone else on this planet. Maybe adding in new habits seems intimidating. Maybe you cling to your comfort zone because life overwhelms you, and the thought of adding new things makes you cringe because you just don't feel like you have the energy. I get that, because that was once me too. But what if some of these habits that you know would be good for you, but haven't allowed yourself to do, added to your life and didn't subtract from it. I've found that to be true for myself. This has encouraged me to be more intentional with my time. And guess what? These things that are new to you now become part of your regular routine, then become second nature shortly after, just like the rest of your habits. Choose to allow yourself to live an enriched life that brings you fulfillment, gives you confidence, has a pace you can flow with, and allows you to embrace your self-care needs. You deserve it; you've always deserved it, and I'm sorry if I'm the first to tell you this. Nonetheless, it's not too late to implement new habits.

This isn't a race to incorporate everything at once. That would probably be more overwhelming than helpful, and I wouldn't necessarily suggest that. However, maybe you can reflect on a couple of new habits every week, or perhaps just one. No matter what pace you set, you can't get this wrong, so please don't feel like a failure if you take on too much or forget to practice these new habits. Everyone has a different set of circumstances, so you will need to do what feels right for you. This is about opening your mindset to new possibilities.

It's helpful to have a flexible approach when adjusting and trying out new routines. You may have to experience some trial and error at first to see which new habits feel good to you. Try out things, get to know what *you* like, and when you figure out what feels good, love yourself enough to make those things a priority. Maybe over the course of this next year, you patiently try out new things slowly but surely and begin to implement your new lifestyle changes at a manageable pace. Then, moving forward, you'll have a beautiful archive of self-care tools and routines that you can give yourself permission to enjoy long term, almost like a recipe book for your well-being. Maybe it's you paying attention to the "callings" you've always felt that say, "I've always wanted to do _____ ." Maybe in those moments it's about creating space for the *why not?* Why not try to find a way to make it happen? Why haven't you allowed yourself to pursue this?" Chances are, if you have a strong interest in something or feel a nudge to try something new, this isn't an accident; it is something you should give yourself the gift of exploring. This is what life is about—honoring these calls and living life to the fullest.

Working Through Resistance

For some, I understand this topic is uncomfortable. You may have even convinced yourself of things such as, "I just don't have the time. There aren't enough hours in the day." "I would rather pour that energy into other people or work projects," or "I just don't enjoy doing things for myself." This may require a deeper look as to why you feel that way and what beliefs are hidden behind these thoughts you hold. For example, maybe you're a mom or dad and you could easily fill up your whole day showing up for your children in beautiful and loving ways. I think it's important to realize that just because you can easily get swayed into this pattern of neglecting your own needs and pouring out all your love to your family, that it's not necessarily the "only way" or the "right way" to handle things. Your children would benefit from watching Mom or Dad take care of themselves. By doing so, you are being a role model and showing your children that they, too, deserve self-care, to live a life they feel passionate about, and to not feel guilty about tending to their own needs.

If the issue is, "I don't enjoy doing nice things for myself," that could be a deeper problem. Perhaps you don't enjoy self-care activities because this is such a foreign concept to you. It may even make you feel uncomfortable or shameful, like you don't deserve it, or you could be thinking, *There are more efficient things I can be spending my time on.* If this is you, that's okay. Admitting the truth is the first step. Maybe your self-worth is tied up in your performance or what you can do for others. This could be deeply rooted in your upbringing, for example, and how you were taught to receive love, by perhaps doing or achieving. There is no shame in having these struggles if this is something that resonates with you. It's just an area to shine some light on and to reflect on with grace. Sometimes the things that are best for you feel the most uncomfortable if it's something you aren't used to. It's so easy to equate the "this is uncomfortable and feels weird" sensation with the belief of "this must be wrong if I feel this way." Sometimes, the habits that are the best for us feel the worst until we further acclimate to them. In terms of giving yourself permission, here are some examples: "I give myself permission to take piano lessons once a week and learn a new instrument for the sheer fun of it." "I give myself permission to go on weekly date nights and get a sitter because my partner and I truly enjoy quality time together." "I ask for help even though I am technically capable of doing something on my own because doing so helps me feel less overwhelmed and burnt out." "I give myself permission to spend a few extra minutes each morning to get ready or be active because it makes me feel grounded and more positive throughout my day." Only you know what those special things are that could bring you more happiness. Maybe you don't necessarily know what they are yet, but I do know that if you spent some time in reflection, you would soon find out. My message to you is this: Please give yourself permission to show up for yourself in new and beautiful ways. And when, or if, you fall into complacency again, forgive yourself and regrant yourself loving permission as many times as you need to. You deserve an abundant life just as much as anyone else; you are no different in that respect. Give yourself permission to nourish yourself and blossom in new and inspiring ways.

Romanticize Your Life

Something I had to give myself permission to do was to romanticize my life. What I mean by this is I had to start taking the time to appreciate my day-to-day experiences, even if they are seemingly mundane. Chances are, there are small moments in your daily life that are valuable to your happiness. And if there aren't, it isn't too hard to incorporate some. This could be as simple as lighting a candle each morning as you get ready and putting on a playlist that sets the tone for your day. This could be waking up a little earlier and taking a few extra minutes to enjoy your morning coffee without distractions. This could be taking the time to appreciate sunrises or sunsets each day and embracing the different color palette each day has to offer. This could be getting dressed in your favorite outfits and taking yourself out on fun little dates. The point is, there are plenty of opportunities to celebrate the little things in life each day, but we have to slow down and be intentional enough to either create them or appreciate them in their fullness. This is when you *truly start living* because you aren't constantly waiting for the *next moment*. You are appreciating the beauty of the moment in front of you *right now*. We don't know how many days we have on this earth, so it's best we honor each passing day as the special gift that it is rather than slipping into autopilot.

Mini Exercise

I want you to spend some time reflecting on things you wish you did, wish you had, or perhaps things you secretly envy about someone else's life. It's no mistake that you feel this way about "those" things, because there's something inside of you that longs for something similar. The secret is to give yourself permission and to work through any limiting beliefs that are holding you back. I would encourage you to have a little fun with this by doing a quick free-style brainstorm session in your phone notes, in a journal, or on a random piece of printer paper, and jot down things that excite you or appeal to you. Now, practice being solution-oriented and challenge yourself to think of fun, creative ways that would allow for this to happen. And if you're still experiencing a deeper resistance to this concept of giving yourself permission, please take a little time to journal and reflect upon why you might feel negatively about showing up for yourself in new ways. (There is no wrong answer here.) Give yourself the space to explore the reasons you deny yourself *permission.* It's never too late to start doing something new. I can give you permission all day long, but it's you who will need to believe it and live it out. I hope you love yourself enough to allow for new and beautiful changes to take place in your life. Let go of fear, and embrace this challenge with a gentle curiosity. It's okay if it takes some time to implement these new habits.

13

The Real Glow Up Is When . . .

You Ground Yourself in Your Spiritual Beliefs

My spiritual practice has been instrumental in those "unknown" and "in between" moments (which are frequent throughout life). Surrendering the things I do not have control over to a higher power is a huge part of my spiritual practice. Some people believe in God; others have faith in the Universe or Source. Some believe in spirit guides, guardian angels, or mother nature running her course. The recurring theme here is that when you believe in a higher power, you are choosing to trust that there is a force stronger and wiser than you, one you can lean on in times of uncertainty. It's impossible to have all the answers, and that's okay; we aren't meant to.

The beauty of a spiritual practice is peace. Peace in the unknown, in the waiting, in the hardship, in not knowing the bigger picture. Peace to me also means strength; for when we are at peace, we are able to be strong in the face of unknown circumstances. I don't think it's any secret that life can come with its fair share of challenges and moments that shake us to the core and make us question all we previously knew before. These moments can be viewed as incredible learning opportunities that shape us in new ways and strengthen our character. When you believe in a higher power, you are able to embrace the fact that the answers will be revealed to you in perfect time, without the need to obsess, allowing things to unfold organically.

The moments I've needed to rely on my spiritual practice the most are in these unknown seasons. Not having full control over my life is a terrifying thought to me. Control is a coping mechanism I've always been drawn to naturally. (Even if control is somewhat of an illusion, I cling to it dearly.) When challenges do present themselves without fully revealing why or how I need to work through them, I find myself desperately searching for where to file these mysterious and often taxing life events. When I'm able to file them in the "I know there is a hidden purpose in this even if I don't understand it right now" folder, I am able to find peace in the confusion and uncertainty of it all. I am able to surrender a little bit more. It's not always easy; in fact, it rarely ever is. But I have gotten into the habit of knowing when to let go and trust in a higher power, even if I have to continuously remind myself that it's okay to not have all the answers. Life wouldn't be interesting if we always understood everything. There is beauty in watching something unfold naturally.

In regards to a higher power, you may have trouble believing in something that isn't a guarantee. The act of letting go without cold, hard proof that it's safe to surrender requires faith in the unknown. For the skeptics, or for the people who identify as non-believers, I want to share a short story with you that may be helpful. When I was thirteen years old, I attended a church camp. There was a guest pastor who shared something that I felt very connected to. I, too, was a bit of a skeptic, even in my younger years. This guest pastor had reframed things in a way that logically made sense to me, and in a way where I could even get my father (a staunch atheist at the time) to understand the benefits of believing and living your life as if there is a higher power. This pastor challenged us by saying, "Okay, what if there isn't a higher power? Then what?" (He immediately had my full attention.) He went on to explain the amount of peace that can come from believing there is one by allowing us to release our grip and let go of constant fear and anxiety, insinuating that this would be beneficial to someone whether God was real or not. He also went on to share about the loving guidelines that are supposed to make up a spiritual practice, such as treating others kindly, helping people, trying to do the right thing, and keeping our humility intact, and how they remain beneficial regardless of whether God is real or not. It was almost as if he was saying, "What do you have to lose?" This was something that I completely resonated with. I agreed that doing things out of love, patience, and surrender is a beautiful thing no matter what and definitely heeds positive results. So my question to you is: "What do you have to lose by believing there is more to this life than what meets the eye?" I can't think of one thing. Perhaps this will ruffle the ego because we don't like being wrong, but in the big scheme of things, it does no harm. I fully believe in a higher power and that a beautiful afterlife awaits us all. But the approach of "giving this belief a chance" may be a good starting point for someone who is a born skeptic and who just can't seem to get past the idea of having faith in something without tangible proof. I also think it's important for me to share that I do not judge anyone who is skeptical about any of this. I believe that everyone could benefit tremendously from letting go and leaning into a loving practice of surrender. I don't think we can do everything in our own strength all of the time. I believe the act of surrender is a beautiful and necessary key to living a joyful life.

Your Ability to Embrace Vulnerability

At the crux of what we're talking about is how we make sense of and navigate situations where we feel vulnerable. You may think there is power in having all of the answers and maintaining careful control of every little thing, but so much of the magic that happens in life is bred from moments where we are able to embrace our vulnerabilities. Brené

Brown, research professor and popular author and speaker, is an expert on teaching people about how we can view vulnerability in a new light. She has helped redefine the word *vulnerability* in powerful ways that have helped many people better understand its purpose in life. This word is often depicted as weakness, but she has an entirely different view on the matter. In her popular book, *Braving the Wilderness: The Quest for True Belonging and the Courage to Stand Alone*, Brown depicts vulnerability in the following way:

> "The definition of vulnerability is uncertainty, risk, and emotional exposure. But vulnerability is not weakness; it's our most accurate measure of courage. When the barrier is our belief about vulnerability, the question becomes: 'Are we willing to show up and be seen when we can't control the outcome?' When the barrier to vulnerability is about safety, the question becomes: 'Are we willing to create courageous spaces so we can be fully seen?'"

Oftentimes, Brown will pair the word vulnerability with *courage*; "to be vulnerable is to be brave" is the overarching message I take from her work. If we are able to lean into uncomfortable moments, we are able to practice courage in expansive and beautiful ways. When we believe in a higher power, we are leaning into that space of vulnerability by trusting that everything will work out the way it was meant to; that we are safe to surrender. It's the simple act of trusting the beauty of the unknown, so we don't always feel the need to play it safe. The truth is, if you want to live out a full, abundant life, you will be met with vulnerability on a frequent basis. Believing in a higher power requires courage.

Mini Exercise

The next time you're experiencing a discouraging moment, or a confusing moment that requires you to be patient, I encourage you to try releasing these fears to a higher power. You might not even know what to call that higher power at first, and that's okay. You can achieve this by simply choosing to believe that everything will work out for the best, and that there is divine purpose in this moment (uncomfortable or not). You can choose to believe that even though you don't have all the answers available, you are safe to surrender and find peace, even in those seemingly chaotic moments. I can't imagine constantly carrying the burden of feeling like I need to do everything in my own strength all the time, especially when there is this beautiful gift available to us—*the gift of trusting that we do not have to do this all on our own.* That gift is peace, and it's absolutely priceless. Whether you find peace through prayer or through looking up at the big, starry sky at night, I hope you allow yourself this gift.

14

The Real Glow Up Is When . . .

Your Growth Triggers Their Issues

As you evolve and grow as a person, you will likely be met with some unexpected resistance from people in your life. Not everyone will understand your growth. Not everyone will see your progress as something to celebrate. Not everyone will support your new journey. This is often extremely difficult to understand. Why wouldn't all your friends, family, and peers be excited to see you actively living your best life while embracing your new self-love journey? Chances are, if you are a kind and good-hearted person, this is mind-boggling to you. You may even feel hurt and confused, constantly searching your brain to see if you have accidentally done something wrong to deserve this judgmental energy. If you aren't clear on why this is happening, it might even throw you off course and result in you tragically giving up on the goals you've set for yourself so that you don't upset anyone. Please know that this scenario is actually quite common. People tend to get upset for a variety of reasons when you start showing up for yourself in new and loving ways. In this chapter, I will unpack some of the reasons you may be experiencing this resistance and how I suggest you approach these situations so you're not derailed from your beautiful and hard-earned progress.

They Benefited from Your Lack of Boundaries

If you are anything like me, you may be (or have been) somewhat of a people pleaser throughout your life—someone who likes to go with the flow and avoid conflict. Certain personalities tend to thrive off this quality in others and use this to their benefit by taking advantage of your lack of self-confidence or respect. This was a major learning experience that hadn't even dawned on me until a few years ago. The truth is, these types of people feel more powerful when someone is letting them call the shots. They may do things such as put you down in front of others and mask it as a joke. You may even laugh with them so that they don't accuse you of being sensitive, dramatic, or unable to take said joke. Others may laugh with them because they don't realize it was a hurtful jab at your expense, which only adds to your negative beliefs, such as: "If I speak up, I'm the problem." I don't fault you if you've tolerated this type of treatment. Perhaps you never realized this was a harmful dynamic to begin with. Sometimes it takes time to unlearn these harmful patterns. But here's the thing: people whom you have allowed to treat you this way are not going to take kindly to your newfound self-respect and ambition; instead, they are going to meet it with resistance. They use your kindness and willingness to overlook their aggressive tendencies to boost their egos and feel better about themselves. If you're quick to people please, they benefit because this allows for things to always be on their terms. When you change this power dynamic, you are essentially "taking" something from them. They may not consciously view it this way, but they feel uncomfortable around this new you who is advocating for yourself in new and meaningful ways. The simple act of no longer laughing when someone tells a joke at your expense sends a strong message. Experiencing negative feelings about someone saying something rude about you is not a weakness; it shows you have self-respect. These types of people will eventually be less interested in spending time with you if you continue to politely and calmly stick up for yourself and advocate for a more respectful dynamic. Trust me when I say, this works in your benefit. You do not have room for people like this in your life if you want to have a genuine support system. You don't want to be "rowing the boat" while these types of people are secretly "drilling holes" when you aren't looking. There are many people who will be quite good at faking relationships for the mere fact that they want to maintain some level of control over you. I strongly encourage you to start paying attention to these types of relationships in your life. It doesn't matter how long you've known them; they are incredibly damaging to your self-esteem and growth. They are like the weeds that take over your garden. It's oftentimes challenging to wrap your mind around this concept, especially if they are sometimes great to you, as this only creates more confusion. By the way, this hot-and-cold behavior is called *intermittent reinforcement*. This consists of treating you really well, then turning the tables and treating you poorly; it confuses people. It's meant to be disorienting so you doubt your own perception, creating cognitive dissonance. It makes poor treatment seem justified and normal. It makes the *good* feel *extra good* because it's coming from the same person that hurt you. It's almost like you want what you can't have, so when they then give it to you, you are grateful. These types of people will absolutely show resistance when you advocate for yourself. Please pay attention to this trap. Don't let someone like this drag you down or confuse you. You deserve happiness. You are serving nobody by playing small to appease the fragile egos of those who benefit from your insecurities. When I made this shift in my life and identified these unhealthy patterns, it was absolutely life-changing for me. I feel like an entirely new person now that I'm not constantly being dragged down by the people who thrived off of my lack of self-esteem and self-worth. Sure, there may be some growing pains, but your self-respect is worth it. You deserve to be surrounded by people who love and support you in life. Your energy is precious and could definitely be better invested elsewhere than on people who secretly wish for your downfall.

Your Change Is like Holding Up a Mirror

Sometimes when we make positive changes in our lives, whether it be through healing, finding self-love, or just growing as a person in general, we are unknowingly causing another person to self-reflect on the changes they might not be making in their own life. You may be the least judgmental person ever, but it doesn't change the fact that your presence could spark uncomfortable feelings for them. This isn't to say people need to live their lives the same way you do; however, if this change happens to be an area that someone may already feel insecure about (consciously or subconsciously), you are shining light on that insecurity for them without realizing it. No, this is not your fault, but it is good to remember because people who feel this way around you may stop coming around as often, or may act guarded around you for this very reason. This typically stems from their own insecurities, and there is nothing you can do about it. You have to stand firm in who you are and in the decisions you've made regardless of how someone acts around you.

Additionally, there are people who have given up on their own dreams or have convinced themselves their dreams are impossible. You see, when they hear you are making bold, brave, and honest efforts to strive for more, these people may clam up inside. It's as if you're holding up a mirror to them and their insecurities where they see their own shortcomings in your success. Their perception of not being capable of achieving their own dreams feels challenged. They have two options: 1) to feel inspired to maybe pick their dreams back up and to begin again (while choosing to be happy for you), or 2) to pass judgement on your decisions to avoid their inner dialogue of *I'm not good enough*, or *I'm a quitter*. This could come across in several ways. It could be extreme, where this person is never happy for you and is judging your progress behind your back (maybe even rolling their eyes right in front of you). Or it could be less intense, and they just don't seem open to talking about your progress with you. It's almost like they go silent or change the subject quickly when you tell them these dreams and plans because it makes them feel too uncomfortable to cheer for you and learn more. If you have these types of people in your life, the best thing you could do is to not share your plans with them and work quietly so that you aren't discouraged by their lack of interest or support. No one is required to support you, but don't share these goals with others if they can't hold an encouraging space for you.

Change Makes Them Uncomfortable
and Brings Up Deeper Fears

Some people struggle with fear of abandonment, so any major changes can make them feel vulnerable in a relationship. And to be fair, advocating for your goals and making yourself a priority is a major 180 if that's something you never allowed yourself to do. This is a big life change—a beautiful one, yet major nonetheless. Some people are scared and intimidated by the dynamic change in your relationship. Maybe you hold your head higher now. Maybe you have a more confident approach to life. Maybe you aren't scared anymore to speak up and be your true self. Not everyone understands that they, too, could make these incredible changes in their life, and they may feel a lost connection with the safe and familiar dynamic you two once shared. Many times, people will adjust to these changes once they realize 1) you've changed for the better, and 2) no, you aren't going anywhere; you still love them dearly. Only then will they begin to feel safe again in this relationship with you. People who experience these fears often just need some extra time to adjust, and that's okay, as long as they are able to respect you along the way.

They Don't Love Themselves

Some people haven't learned to love themselves, so to watch you radically love *yourself* intimidates and triggers them. Why? Because it's not how they live their lives, so it shakes their perception of what life is like and "should" be like. Quite honestly, it confuses them, which makes them feel threatened. Ideally, we'd love for people to feel inspired to love and prioritize themselves and their goals because there is more than enough room for all of us. However, some people don't understand that. Some people think it's a personal attack on their view of life. Some people truly believe it is selfish to live with self-love. They don't understand the bigger picture that when you are able to show up for yourself, you are better able to show up for others. The hope would be that these people could come around to this "new you" and maybe even adapt a bit by incorporating some self-love into their own lives. But this is complex, and it is not our job to force someone into understanding this truth. Sometimes these relationships just grow apart over time, and that's okay too. You can be encouraging and uplifting, of course, but you can't force them to change their mind. This truth is difficult to accept, but it's a common occurrence in life when two people are on very different life paths and share very different beliefs.

How to Continue Moving Forward Despite
the Resistance of Others

Now that you understand that many of these instances aren't at all personal (even if it feels like it), let's talk about how you can move forward without letting these scenarios derail your progress. For one, you must learn how to let go of people pleasing while learning how to validate yourself. This can sometimes be challenging, especially at the beginning, but it's an incredible skill to acquire that will serve you well throughout your life. You don't need the approval of others to know you are on the right path. You can give that approval to yourself. No one knows what's best for you more than you. Next, you can try to understand what may be happening in these relationships without absorbing others' harsh judgments as truths. When you know it's not personal, you react less, therefore saving more of your energy. You can avoid unnecessary drama by setting healthy boundaries with people and by doing this, you protect yourself from slipping backward into old comfort zones. It's crucial to be mindful of how you limit your exposure to people who aren't supportive of your personal growth. This protects your energy and mindset. At times, it is completely necessary to quit sharing your dreams, goals, and plans with certain people if they judge or belittle your progress. When in doubt, work in silence. Pursuing your dream life and choosing yourself is intimidating enough without a judgmental audience chiming in. Know that it is completely safe to be yourself and to live life on your own terms. Some will certainly try to convince you this is selfish, but remember that anyone who is a healthy part of your support system would never make you choose between your personal growth and their comfort zone. As mentioned, there are varying levels of this issue. Some people just need time to adjust and warm up to this change; others won't ever support you the way you need them to and will inevitably drag you down if you don't advocate for yourself and set strong boundaries. The reason I bring this topic to your attention is because if you don't know any better, you may think you are doing something wrong. I promise you that you are on the right track if you notice this happening; this resistance is common, as hurtful as it may be. You may have to grieve certain relationships, and you may have to grieve your old way of being too. Be gentle with yourself in the process of letting go of what no longer serves you. The path less traveled is unbelievably worth it, and you will eventually find the people who support you and even inspire you on your own journey (and vice versa).

Mini Exercise

Where you are in your journey and the level of support surrounding you will make a huge difference as to how much this chapter benefits you. It's very easy to feel guilty or confused if you aren't used to advocating for yourself. This topic is crucial for you to be aware of so that you are empowered to navigate these situations appropriately. If you're lucky, you won't have to worry about this too much along the way. Regardless, I want you to be mindful of how people's reactions either leave you feeling encouraged or discouraged. I never want you to feel like this kind of behavior from others is a poor reflection on you. You deserve a life you are proud of. You deserve self-love and to live a joyful, fulfilling life. Please don't let anyone convince you otherwise. I encourage you to pay close attention to the people in your life, and gauge their reactions when you share your goals, visions, and accomplishments with them. Just know that it is easier and more beneficial to have no support on a project or goal than to have people dragging you down. And if no one has told you this yet, I believe in you, and I am so proud of your progress.

Disclaimer: This is not to judge or shame others who cannot support you. Everyone is on their own life path. I simply want you to be aware of how to protect your mindset from unnecessary discouragement.

15

The Real Glow Up Is When . . .

You Feel Confident Enough to "Take Up Space"

Many of us were taught to play according to a certain set of rules: "Do this, but don't do that." "You can speak up, but not too much or you'll seem arrogant." "Do better, but not better than us." "Dream big, but don't chase a fantasy; be realistic." When you're finally able to break the mold of all the expectations set upon you, then the magic can finally take place. If you subscribe to what is safe and easily acceptable, and you adhere to the plethora of rules, as well as society's expectations of you, I guarantee you will be cheating yourself. Many of us were taught to feel like our dreams were too big, or too wild, or they were for *them* and not *us.* This couldn't be more wrong. No one gets to tell you what your dreams are and what you are capable of; *you* decide that.

Embarking on this journey of stepping into your fullest potential and most authentic self is going to require you to think differently than you may have before. Once you step into this territory, you will notice not everyone will clap the same way as they would if you followed the rules and achieved a "normal" accomplishment (preapproved by society). For example, when I graduated from college and got hired at the number-one local news station, it felt like many people supported me. Friends and family were constantly complimenting me on my success. But on the flip side, when I first started telling people about my plan to start an online clothing boutique, most people were strangely quiet and seemed confused. It wasn't until much later, when the brand had launched, that people started to see my vision and congratulate me. When I first told people about my plan to write books and become an author, the conversations (in most instances) were a little awkward, as if writing was a silly pipe dream. Does this mean I should make decisions that everyone easily claps for? Or does this mean I need to get comfortable with standing in my own unique power, use my voice in ways that feel authentic to my calling, and pursue a life that feels purposeful and in tune with who I truly am? *This is about being confident enough to take up space.* I'd be cheating myself if I only pursued goals that people could easily cheer for and support. I don't know about you, but when I'm on my deathbed, looking back at my life, I want to say I lived a life that was authentic to who I truly am instead of a safe existence that pleased the status quo of what others deemed as acceptable.

It's intimidating to start taking up space in new ways, whatever it is that you are pursuing. It often feels like there is someone who is better qualified or better suited. In terms of writing and sharing self-love advice, I can easily slip into imposter syndrome. In fact, I struggle with this often and have to constantly remind myself that my life experiences, my unique voice, and the wisdom that I've gained throughout my life are valuable, whether someone agrees with me on that or not. Maybe you struggle to see your value in a certain area too. It's quite common to feel unsafe when showing up in new ways. It's easy to talk ourselves out of something unfamiliar. We tend to be our harshest critic. We may not feel educated enough. We may not feel like we have enough credentials, or a large social media following, or come from a wealthy upbringing (the list goes on and on). Rest assured, you still have value and you still have a unique perspective to share. Tabitha Brown, the famous social media personality, *New York Times* bestselling author, vegan chef, and actress says, "I ain't nobody's chef. I ain't never been to nobody's school. But people hire me like a chef to cook. To tell my story. I ain't never been to nobody's school for public speaking, but yet, I lead panels, conferences, banquets, festivals. I wasn't trained on it, no. But what have I done? I lived. While we live, it builds character, right? And it shapes us into who we are going to become." Tabitha is a huge success and inspiration to so many (including myself). What if she held back from sharing her life experiences and natural-born gifts because she didn't feel qualified enough? She qualified herself and believed in her life-earned wisdom. She didn't listen to critics and "play it safe" to please others (and thank God for that). Tabitha is the perfect example of what it means to believe in yourself, take a less conventional approach (that may be less accepted by others at the beginning), and now she is a living picture of success. What do I take from this? Qualify *yourself.* Don't look to others to validate your dreams or your level of competence, and don't be surprised if people don't clap for you until much later, when you have already proven you are successful. At this point, that's the world we live in—not everyone can see your vision. If you're lucky, you will have some supportive people in your corner through all stages of this process, but if you don't, please don't view that as a reflection of your value or your ability to achieve your dreams.

The reason I saved this chapter for the back end of this book is because you can build your solid foundation on self-love. You can get super clear on what you're passionate about and where you feel your talents could best flourish. You can have a specific plan in place and be truly enthusiastic about it. But oftentimes, it feels scary or counterintuitive to allow yourself to "take up space," stand in your power, and believe in yourself enough to move forward with your goals. It's important to know that no matter what you do in life, not everyone will support you along the way, and that's okay. It can feel really scary to bet on yourself and push through fear while pursuing a nonconventional dream or goal. Just because it can feel scary or intimidating does not mean you should give up or water down your dreams.

It's crucial to realize that even if the risk feels big to try something new, oftentimes we are just fearful of rejection or judgment, which isn't actually as harmful as it may seem. It is brave to put yourself out there and try something different. You are never a failure by simply believing in yourself enough to take action on something. This risk of rejection isn't an end-all-be-all scenario. You are allowed to learn, experiment, create, pivot, and do whatever it takes to embody your fullest self in this life. Once we can get past this fear, we make space for the big, bright, creative, and unique ideas to take form. I don't know about you, but gone are the days where I am playing it safe and denying myself of pursuing what lights me up inside and makes me feel alive. If this upsets someone else, or if it makes someone cringe, that is not my burden to bear any longer. I hope you, too, have the courage to take up space in this world, applause or not.

Disclaimer: The more your goal deviates from neatly packaged societal norms and expectations, the more resistance you will face. As long as you fully believe in what you're sharing with the world and think it could help others, keep at it anyway. Please do not let small-minded people discourage you. Someone needs what you have to offer.

Mini Exercise

I think this is a timely opportunity to jot down some of the "big and bold" dreams you have (or have had) for your life. Perhaps ones that you haven't even entertained before because you know it would require you to cheer yourself on and face potential rejection or judgment along the way. *Those* dreams, the ones that your heart quietly longs for but your mind quickly sweeps under the rug. The ones that if you were on your deathbed, you would always wonder, *What if I had believed in myself and actually went for it?*

Now, I think it's important to be honest with yourself about what fears these bring up for you and why you feel unqualified or incapable of pursuing them. Oftentimes, our fears aren't actually as scary as they seem; they simply require you to step out of your comfort zone and believe in yourself. Bringing your dreams and fears into the light will help you make sense of why you are holding yourself back. And perhaps it may reveal why you actually *are* capable of pursuing these dreams. Remember: you are safe to take up space in this world.

16

The Real Glow Up Is When . . .

You Tap into Your Resilience

Throughout these chapters, I detail how you can get in touch with the softer, more vulnerable side of yourself through self-love practices—and that's a beautiful and worthwhile achievement. However, something I noticed on my own journey is that regardless of how much you heal and embrace your softness, you will be put in situations where you need to tap into your resilient nature (a less soft and more rugged side of yourself). You will need to combine these two forces in order to make it in this life, to reach your full potential, and to overcome setbacks. There is beauty in these opposing character traits, and they are complimentary when fully understood and integrated. The thing is, there are moments in life where we may hit a proverbial wall (or several), and it can cause us to lose our sense of direction and our hope for the future. You might feel like a victim of your circumstances and want to give up on your goals entirely. I can say this because I've felt this to my core. However, these are the defining moments where you can either lose yourself completely, or you can choose to tap into the resilient side within you (because we all have it). In fact, resilience is so inherent we are actually *born with it*, we just tend to forget that. Popular author and speaker Mel Robbins has talked about this topic. She shares about how babies learn to crawl, to stand up, and eventually walk. When they fall, they continue to get up again and again—not giving up until their goal is accomplished. Sure, it helps if the baby has a healthy support system in the process, but as babies we had this undeniable grit deep down inside of us at such a tender age—and it's still there. It will always live inside of you. It's something you can rely on whenever you need to, but it's your choice whether you do. Sometimes we just need to remind ourselves of our capabilities and strength. Below, I'll share some advice for how you can activate yours.

Practicing Acceptance

As mentioned, it's easy to fall into the victim mindset when we face struggles. It can be disheartening when you work so hard for a goal to no avail, or when you are hit with a massive setback in life. This can feel unfair, confusing, and like we are being kicked when we are already down. I know this feeling deeply, and mentally; it's a dark place to reside. It can strip you of your hope and faith in this world and can rock your belief system entirely. I went through my own version of this recently. I had remained dedicated and patient while working toward a few important goals that I hold close to my heart, and eventually I felt so discouraged because I had seemingly nothing to show for it after almost two years of hard work. I questioned why this was happening. I felt stuck, stagnant, confused, and even hopeless at times. It made me feel like I wasn't cut out for this. I hated that I felt like a victim, especially because I knew there were so many positive aspects to my life in the midst of my issues. I knew much worse could be happening, but it didn't change how I felt about my circumstances. It was a cycle I knew I had to finally break. I then went searching for answers and came across the topic of resilience. Specifically, I found a TED Talk by Lucy Hone, a professional speaker and award-winning academic, who had faced her own tragedy in life when her thirteen-year-old daughter was killed in a car accident. Lucy said something that really helped me break out of my victim mindset: "Resilient people *get* that shit happens. They know that suffering is a part of life. This doesn't mean they welcome it in, they're not actually delusional. Just that, when the tough times come, they seem to know that suffering is part of every human existence." When she said this, it helped free me from my victim mindset. It was as if something finally clicked. My problems are not special; they are simply a part of the human existence. Now, does that mean I expect things to go wrong in my life from now on? No, but when setbacks strike, I'm no longer going to sit around thinking, *Why me?* because I now understand that suffering is a part of the human experience; it's unavoidable. Ultimately, this is a lesson in acceptance. This encourages us to focus on what we can control, rather than obsess over what we cannot.

It's important to touch on how the current culture of social media contributes to the overall feeling of *I am failing in life if I am not happy and successful.* We are conditioned to share the highlights of our life, myself included. The problem with this is, through social media, we often aren't getting an accurate portrayal of what life is really like for people, and this is clouding our judgment and our perception about what life "should" look like. I say this because you may need to remind yourself that it is completely normal to struggle, and you aren't alone in it just because you don't see that represented in your social media feeds. People of all walks of life are experiencing issues whether they broadcast them online, or not. So please use discernment when scrolling these apps. They are not an accurate representation of real life.

Make Peace with Your Circumstances

The truth is, no matter how much we wish we didn't have to endure a situation, dwelling on the negative will not do anything but keep you stuck in the past. Stuck in a moment where you pictured things being different from what they are now. While your feelings are always valid, it's important you maintain a healthy mindset as well. It's easy to get attached to the old expectations we became so familiar with. Unfortunately, whatever you are going through will not change, no matter how much you "stomp your feet" and feel bad for yourself. (Please know, I say this with love because I needed to hear this at one point too.) It is critical to make peace with yourself and your circumstances, trusting that the life you've been given is not a punishment. It is okay to grieve the original life you had planned, but at a certain point it isn't healthy to resist the grieving process and cling to the past. Assess your struggle, and kindly remind yourself that you are here now. You can only move forward, not backward (no matter how much that may sting). Try your best to not fight the present moment because the present is all you truly have. It causes us great anguish to live in the past because we have no control over what happened. We can only respond to our current circumstances accordingly. Please be gentle with yourself and make space to process whatever messy feelings arise while you learn to make peace with your circumstances. You will make it through this. You are much stronger than you realize.

Find Your Sense of Humor

Have you ever heard someone say, "Laughter is the best medicine"? There is a reason this has become a popular saying. It isn't just another form of toxic positivity; there's some actual science behind it. Laughter is your body's way of coping with stressful situations because it releases endorphins and dopamine, which helps you instantly feel a little better and helps to cultivate a more positive attitude. There are certainly going to be moments where this is tougher to do, but the more often we can find humor in our day-to-day life, the more we provide levity to difficult situations. Tapping into our sense of humor gives us more energy to move through these tough seasons of life, even if it feels counterintuitive.

Refuse to Give Up

Whether you are going through a personal hardship or you are striving for an important goal that feels impossible (or perhaps both scenarios at once), it is critical you make a commitment to not give up. Remove that option from your mind entirely. When you take away this option, you are better able to focus on your goal without wavering. That being said, you may need to take breaks along the way—to rest rather than to quit—and that's perfectly normal. But if you know in your heart that this is something you'd like to overcome, then you have to remove *giving up* from your vocabulary. When I feel like quitting, I like to remind myself of some of the inspiring success stories where people overcame (what seemed like) insurmountable obstacles. This is helpful because when you find yourself in the midst of a serious challenge, or in a difficult season in life, some of your goals may seem impossible to achieve (this is especially true the longer you've been pursuing them). Below, I'll share some examples of success stories I find inspiration in.

Bethany Hamilton, Professional Surfer

Bethany Hamilton was passionate about surfing and started at the young age of three. Unfortunately, she was tragically bitten by a shark when she was only thirteen, resulting in her losing an arm. One may assume her surfing career was over, but she didn't let this massive setback stop her from reaching her goals. Against all odds, she persevered, going on to win huge championships. The 2011 film *Soul Surfer* chronicles her journey and how she summoned the courage to overcome the many obstacles and fears she faced while building a successful surfing career. She is now a mother, a writer, and a sought-after motivational speaker.

Nelson Mandela, Activist

Nelson Mandela, the well-known South African leader, was
incarcerated due to political persecution for twenty-seven years of his
life (much of which was spent in a high-security prison). He could
have let this sentencing knock him down and accept defeat, but he did
just the opposite; he was only more determined to work toward the
justice he was after. He continued to oppose apartheid, which was a
system of legislation that upheld racial segregation against non-white
citizens of South Africa. Once released from prison, Mandela helped
to negotiate an end to apartheid and went on to become the first
democratically elected president of South Africa. While in prison, he
famously kept a note with the lines from Henley's poem "Invictus"
that read: "*I am the master of my fate: I am the captain of my soul.*"

Keanu Reeves, Actor

Many know Keanu Reeves for his numerous roles, such as the hit
movie series *The Matrix*, but they may be surprised to know the
struggles he endured before his career success. At the age of seventeen,
he was depressed and dropped out of school, moving to Hollywood
shortly thereafter. Things were seemingly going well. He found a new
girlfriend, she got pregnant, and they were excited to start a family
together. Well, things quickly started to crash in his life when their
baby died at eight months old. And just a year-and-a-half later, his
girlfriend died as well. Keanu could have given up and let this derail all
of this plans, but he chose not to. Despite the tragedy, he continued to
live out a successful career and eventually found love again.

Oprah Winfrey, TV Host

Oprah Winfrey grew up in the inner city of Milwaukee, Wisconsin. She grew up poor and was both mistreated and sexually abused. She even became pregnant from one of the assaults as a young teen, but it resulted in a miscarriage. Oprah could have let the tragedies of her life consume her; instead, she went on a journey of healing, self-discovery, and empowerment. She entered the world of journalism and overcame countless obstacles as a woman of color. Through her dedication, she eventually went on to become one of the most inspiring celebrities in the world, hosting a show which reaches millions of viewers. She used her early trauma as a tool to tap into her compassion and strength.

I don't know about you, but these four stories are so inspiring they give me goose bumps. They all display resilience at its finest. When your hope is dwindling, I encourage you to look up stories like these. They may help you realize the importance of not giving up.

Get Clear on Your Purpose

Get in the habit of asking yourself, "Why do I want to accomplish this goal?" or "Why is it important for me to overcome this?" Is it critical to your well-being and survival? Is it a lifelong passion of yours? Does this goal have the potential to help someone (or several people)? Only *you* can determine the purpose behind this goal, but it's important to get clear on your why so that when you have moments of doubt, confusion, or overwhelm, you can remind yourself why you started. This clarity will supply the grit you need to endure the journey ahead.

Believe in Yourself

At the end of the day, you need to believe in yourself, even if no one else does. In fact, it is more important to have self-belief than it is to have a group of people cheering you on. Sure, it would be a comforting feeling to have that level of support, but if you had to choose between one or the other, one is crucial to your resilience and the other is an added bonus. And remember, even when you have confidence in yourself and your capabilities, it is completely normal to face moments of self-doubt and insecurity. You can respond to these moments with self-compassion or with positive affirmations. You can choose to think new thoughts and speak kindly to yourself in the midst of uncertainty. To cheer yourself on like you would a loved one. Bottom line, the single most important thing you can do is to root for yourself, to believe in yourself, and to never give up on yourself.

Summary

I get that life can feel unfair. We can work so hard to accomplish our goals, to heal our inner wounds, to actively strive for a life we've always dreamed of, only to feel like we are further behind than when we started. I've been there. I've sat in these feelings of utter confusion and frustration, and it feels deeply personal, lonely even. But can I tell you something? Struggle does not have to be how your story ends. You can change the narrative at any time. How do you do this? By controlling what you can and by making peace with what you can't. Also, get clear on your purpose. Believe in yourself regardless if others join you. Choose to rest rather than quit. Remember that social media isn't an accurate depiction of life. Tap into your sense of humor when you can. Remember that struggle is an unavoidable part of the human existence. Finally, choose to not give up.

Mini Exercise

Have you been experiencing frustration around certain goals due to a lack in progress? Has it caused you to give up or perhaps pull back a bit on your efforts? It can be so easy to fall into a funk with certain goals when we don't see any progress, and our pursuits might begin to feel stale overtime. We may even fall into a state of "learned helplessness," which occurs when a person has experienced a stressful situation repeatedly, causing them to believe that they are unable to change or control the situation, and so they fall into a pattern of not trying anymore, even when opportunities or solutions arise. This typically shows up as a lack of self-esteem, low motivation, a lack of dedication, and ultimately failure to reach goals. (Falling into this state is even more common when one has experienced child abuse or domestic violence). If you identify with this description of learned helplessness, it is nothing to be ashamed of. It is just something to be aware of. Awareness is key in moving past this. We can do so by getting into the habit of simply observing our thoughts around certain goals. Are you noticing a negative thought pattern? Are you remaining open to looking into potential solutions? Are you feeding yourself empowering thoughts about yourself and your situation? Are there any subconscious beliefs stemming from an event in your life that makes you feel inferior or incapable of completing something? Is this something you can show yourself compassion about and keep in mind while you move forward so you can rewrite these narratives? I encourage you to journal in response to these questions if this scenario feels applicable to you.

I promise that you are inherently resilient, even if you have to unlearn some patterns along the way.

17

The Real Glow Up Is When . . .

You Are Kind and Give Back to Others

The truth is, I believe in you. I believe you will find success, fulfillment, healing, and live out your very best life—as long as you are bold enough to believe in yourself along the way. That's why this final chapter is important for me to share with you. It was a chapter that hadn't dawned on me until one random night when I was tossing and turning in bed. I quickly rushed to write down some notes in my phone because I knew just how important and powerful this component is to living a full, vibrant, and beautiful life. Throughout these chapters, my goal is to empower you to live a life you're proud of. It's important to prioritize your needs without feeling guilty or selfish. However, it's undeniable that giving back to others is a critical facet in living a healthy and well-balanced life. This could mean helping people through your work; being open to mentoring people who are inspired by you; using your influence, platform, or leadership to advocate for marginalized groups; intentionally making an effort to give to charities (within your means, of course), and maintaining a giving spirit rather than an "only living for yourself" mentality.

I believe that the people who live the fullest of lives have so much to give, and a responsibility to do so. It would be such a shame to live with a greedy, all-mine mindset and to hold back from others. Not only would this be a disadvantage for others to never receive your help or assistance, but it's a disadvantage for you as well. Because when we give, we actually receive. In fact, an article published by the Greater Good Science Center speaks to why it feels so good to give:

> "These good feelings are reflected in our biology. In a 2006 study, Jorge Moll and colleagues at the National Institutes of Health found that when people give to charities, it activates regions of the brain associated with pleasure, social connection, and trust, creating a "warm glow effect.""

Did you catch that? The way our brains become activated with feel-good chemicals when we help others creates a "warm glow effect," also known as "the real glow up." When you aren't operating from a giving mentality, you are cheating yourself out of a beautiful, shared experience. When you have an opportunity to help others (within your means), I hope you lean toward a giving mentality more often than not. I don't suggest you run yourself into the ground for others. That would deviate from everything I've shared in this book. I still wholeheartedly believe you cannot pour from an empty cup; therefore in order to effectively give to others, you need to be taking care of yourself first. And I still believe we need to set appropriate boundaries with people who may take advantage of our kindness. However, the act of giving back is extraordinarily important in the larger picture of life, and I hope you identify as a giver and not someone who operates out of a place of fear and lack. I promise that no matter where you are in your life (financially, spiritually, socially, emotionally), you have the ability to help others. It could be as simple as a two-dollar donation to a charity, a quickly signed petition, a creative and intentional idea such as a clothing drive or a bake sale to benefit a good cause, or perhaps volunteering for a local nonprofit. Each small action counts. You don't need to overcomplicate things in order to make a difference. For example, if you see someone in front of you in line at the grocery store who can't afford all their groceries, and they need to put a few items back, then if it is within your means to help, please offer to do so. It's best to live by the golden rule, which states: "Treat others how you would like to be treated." Also, please do this from your heart and not to gain praise or attention from others. I promise you it will make you feel more connected to people when you're giving for the right reasons.

I leave you with this parting note doused with love, support, and encouragement for you on your journey. Please, by all means, live out your life to your fullest potential. Start by building a solid foundation. Learn to love yourself compassionately and radically. Pursue your dreams, give yourself permission, but always rest when you need to. Take risks that are in line with your goals, validate yourself, qualify yourself, and embrace life fully on your own terms. But also, when you see someone who could genuinely use a helping hand and you have the means to do so, please consider lending yours.

This is the real glow up.

For my husband, who has unconditionally loved and supported me throughout this journey of healing. It wasn't always easy, and I often had to break down completely to build myself up, but you always believed in me before understanding or ever seeing the bigger picture. Thank you for always giving me the space to unapologetically be myself and to carve out my own path. Your unwavering love and support means the world to me.

C H E L S E Y A R M F I E L D was born and raised in Washington State, just outside of Seattle, and currently resides there with her husband and dog. She graduated from the University of Washington with a bachelor's degree in Media Communications, with a focus on journalism. Although her career endeavors have been incredibly diverse, she has ultimately discovered her true passion lies in self-love advocacy and writing. Her writing is inspired from real-life experiences, which have without a doubt shaped her path, while also providing valuable life lessons. She feels passionate about sharing this wisdom with others so they, too, can heal through self-love and go onto live out their fullest life. For more books and for social media information visit: C H E L S E Y A R M F I E L D . C O M

Made in United States
Troutdale, OR
09/18/2023

12978537R00096